Confessions of the Perfect Mom:
Baby And Toddler Years

Kat Ryan

© 2015 Kat Ryan

All Rights Reserved.

No part of this publication may be reproduced, stored in a retrieval system, or transmitted, in any form or by any means, electronic, mechanical, photocopying, recording, or otherwise, without the written permission of the author.

First published by Dog Ear Publishing
4011 Vincennes Rd
Indianapolis, IN 46268
www.dogearpublishing.net

ISBN: 978-1-4575-3902-2

This book is printed on acid-free paper.

Printed in the United States of America

I dedicate this book to my amazing husband. Without his support, this book would never have been completed. Thank you for supporting me in the crazy process.

I also dedicate it to my girls. Without them and their stories, I would not have had the inspiration or, frankly, the material to write this.

Contents

Introduction 1
1. Becoming Mommy 3
2. The Big Day 7
3. Initiation: The First Six Weeks 24
4. Poo (Because Yes, It Does Deserve Its Own Chapter) 34
5. Breastfeeding 39
6. Learning to Speak 45
7. Temper Tantrums 48
8. The Insanity Starts Again: Adding a Sibling 53
9. Potty Training 66
10. Let the Rivalry Begin 78
11. Insanity All Over: Adding a Third to the Mix 84
12. Surviving Your First Emergency 101
13. Be the A-Team: Be the Awesome Team 109
14. Happy Moments 115

Introduction

I am going to start by saying I am not a child psychologist. I do not have a college degree on childhood development or early education. If you are wanting to read a book by someone with those credentials, then this is not the book for you; however, if you are wanting to read stories with humor, advice, and just a sense of not being alone, then keep on going.

I started this by telling all of the things that I am not. Now I want to take a moment to tell you a bit about the things that I am. At nineteen, I married the love of my life (and no, I was not pregnant, as many, many, many people incorrectly assumed). The next year, we had our first of three daughters. My husband and I own a not-so-small business that has provided us an amazing life. With this, I have had the joys (and the tears) of being a working mom, a work-from-home mom, and a stay-at-home mom, all of which were equally hard in their own way. I had the ability to do a different one with each of my girls. No wonder they all turned out so incredibly different.

My friends often poke fun at me being "the perfect mom"—hence the name of my book. Yes, I am that mom who does it all. My hair and makeup are always done, my kids are always dressed, I bake, I craft, I homeschool my girls, I am patient, my kids are always well-behaved and polite. From the outside, it looks like my feathers are never ruffled and everything is... well, perfect. Let me assure you this is just the face I show to the outside world. Every mother goes through the same embarrassing moments, and all of our kids have some of the same issues. Some of us are just better at hiding it.

Now that you know a bit about me, let's start with this crazy thing we call motherhood.

CHAPTER 1

Becoming Mommy

There was a night a few weeks back that, hopefully, was a lot of fun—or, in my case, involved lots of adult beverages. Yes, this did happen to be the case for all three pregnancies, and even though that might seem kinda reckless, or unplanned, all three girls were planned. (My hubby says that we were just no longer preventing. I say if you are not preventing, you are trying. But who is splitting hairs?)

Good ole Aunt Flow is delayed, which she never is. She is that more-than-annoying, right-on-time family member who comes whether she is welcome or not. So you test. If you are lucky, you get an answer right away; other times, it takes a few more days (or weeks, like the case with my youngest—should have known she was going to be her own girl right then and there). But whenever that test tells you you're pregnant, your world is forever changed in ways that you cannot even begin to imagine.

With our first, we got that positive test right away, and I was beyond excited. If memory serves me right, I even jumped into my husband's arms. We were young and had no idea what we were in for. We were simply thrilled to be starting our little family. We immediately went out and bought all of the

What to Expect-type books and began reading everything that we could get our hands on.

For our second, I went to the doc to get some routine blood work done for other health items. [Nothing serious, so no need to worry about me (or baby).] They ran a pregnancy test, just as precaution, with it. I laughed when they had me sign saying it was okay. As far as I thought, the timeline didn't line up and there was "no possible way that I am pregnant." That was the exact line that I told the doc. Our general practice doc called me at about 7:00 that same night. Our doc keeps normal office hours, so I was terrified when I saw that number come up, because docs (1) don't call that fast with good news and (2) certainly don't call after office hours with good news. Right? I swore I was doomed. I yelled over to my husband that the doctor was calling me, and he immediately rushed into my office, sat down in the chair opposite my desk, and waited for the impending doom that was the doctor's phone call.

My doctor cheerfully answered my tentative hello with "Congratulations! You're pregnant!"

I sat down and took an entire minute to respond, "Are you sure?" Silly me, I know. Remember that not-so-small business that I mentioned in the intro? (Oh, you didn't read the intro? Go back and read it. I'll wait. Okay now that you have read it, do you remember that not-so-small business that I mentioned?) We were still at the office working, with a large portion of our staff. Since I was in disbelief that I was actually pregnant, I didn't want to tell my husband and risk someone overhearing. I wrote, "I am Pregnant," on a sticky note to pass over to my husband. He responded, "No really, what did the doctor say?" I just pointed to the note. His response: "How did that happen?" I gave him that look—you know, the one that says not to be a dumbass. His response: "Well, next week, if you are late we can take another test. Just to make sure." Needless to say, I took the news a bit better than he did.

Our third, however, is a completely different story. We made the decision to have a third, maybe try for a boy. (Well, my husband wanted a boy. Secretly, I knew I wanted another girl.) We stopped preventing, then about two weeks later, I changed my mind. We had two amazing little girls, and that was enough for me. I just needed good old Aunt Flow to say hi, and I would get back on the pill. She did a no-show, not very nice of her, so I tested. Test one = negative. Whew, I was a bit relieved! Went about my day. A week or so went by and still no Aunt Flow. Now this old biddy was getting rude. But being the responsible girl that I am, I tested again. Test two = negative. Hmm. I was beginning to wonder what was going on. Concerned but not worried, I went about my day.

A few days later, we were holding our annual charity event for our not-so-small business. For this, we have all of our employees come into the office with all of their families (wives, children, significant others, the kid down the block who could use a reminder about charity—everyone was invited, the more the merrier). Then after the event, we host our annual holiday party. It has a reputation for being a wild good time. Knowing that this was the night ahead of us and that I was going to be drinking heavily, I thought that I should test one more time since old Aunt Flow was refusing to show up at her scheduled time. Test number three = bingo positive. I was thrilled, then completely and utterly panicked.

I dropped everything, loaded both kids, who were still in their pajamas, into the car, and raced to the office. My mascara was running all over my red puffy face, I was hysterical. Crying, blubbering, on the verge of hyperventilating. I really was a mess. My poor husband's face when I came in... He must have thought someone had died. I choked out, "I'm pregnant." He laughed at me.

That's right, he actually laughed at his hysterical pregnant wife. When he finally calmed down a bit, he smiled and said, "Congratulations. You better get a bit cleaned up and find the kids some shoes." Okay, he handled that one better.

No matter how *you* choose to celebrate—or panic—about becoming a mother, it will be a memory that you will never forget. It gets etched in there right along with every other important memory. And no matter how you react, it will be the right way for you. Just because you are a total panicked mess the first time does not mean you will be for the next one (if you choose to have more than one). Or if you are the calm, happy, excited mommy-to-be the first round but a crying, scared ball of nerves for the next, it does not mean that there is anything wrong. It is okay and, frankly, perfectly normal, to have a different reaction with each baby. Each baby is going to be different, and with that will bring about a whole host of different emotions for you. Enjoy the ride; it is just getting started.

(Most people would now have lots of funny stories about pregnancy, but that is a whole book in and of itself. Let's skip to the main event....labor and delivery.)

CHAPTER 2

The Big Day

Woo hoo, we survived pregnancy. Some more gracefully than others, but the point is, we all survived. Yea, us! When that big day arrives, there is much emotion and many things going through our minds. *Will I be a good mom?* was always the first thought in my head. Followed closely by *How will I provide for this baby?* and *What have I gotten myself into?* And then it hit me: *How much will this hurt?* I am a total wimp when it comes to pain. I can admit this, or better, I can own this. I do not like pain, in any shape or form. That last thought came screaming up to the front of my mind like a freight train. Then screamed at me for most of the pregnancy.

All of my babies were scheduled and evicted. I know, I'm off to a bad start on this motherhood train by not letting nature take its course and having them come when they were ready. In my defense, at least with the last two, it was better that I picked the date so I could make sure that the other girls were watched and I was not racing around, trying to find a last-minute sitter. Less stress for me means less stress for the baby, and that is a good thing. Also, I would get to plan it on a day that *my* OB was on call. I didn't want some strange man I had never met before calling the shots and down in my business while I was so exposed. Not going to happen. My doc knew me, knew how I wanted this to go down. That was a much, much better plan. Again, less stress for me means less stress for baby. So see, my intentions were the best all the way around.

Why, oh why, does the hospital make the time to start this party be between 2:00 and 4:00 AM? We are pregnant women, tired, stressed, emotional, and getting ready to go through the absolutely hardest thing that we will ever go through, both physically and emotionally. One would think that they would let me try to get one last full night of sleep, but nope, with all three of my girls, my husband and I were there well before the sun was up. I think it must be their way to punish those poor pregnant women who choose to evict their babies. After what feels like an eternity and a mountain of paperwork, I am finally taken back. There is this excitement that this is going to start. Ha-ha, funny thought. Nope, the nurses then want to review that entire mountain of paperwork, without baby daddy in the room. I know they do this to provide a safe place for women who need it. I truly respect them for that and for the women speaking up in that moment. I did not need it, I was ready to get going, and it seemed like forever to go over it all again.

Then the poking and prodding starts. Good nurses can do this all on the first try, with hardly any pain. The rest, I think, enjoy poking people more than once. This is just a hunch, of course; I have no proof to back it up, and certainly, no nurse will ever admit this, but I am still convinced this is the case.

For me, it was at this point that the real fears started to kick in. See, I am terrified of needles. I started crying the moment the needles came into the room. By the time they got near me, I was hyperventilating and couldn't breathe. If I was having a full-on panic attack at just the sight of the stuff needed to start an IV, how was I supposed to expel a human being out of my body through a teeny-tiny passageway? Nope, not going to do it. Baby girl could just stay in there, right where she was. Party over.

Yes, you know women have been doing this since the beginning of time. Yes, you know until recently that they even did it without any pain meds, and your nurses will gently remind you of these facts. A thought went through my mind, and I clung to it with every fiber in my being: *It can't be that horrible, or families would never have more than one child. If women choose to have more than one without pain meds, then certainly, I too can do this.* People talk about the miracle of birth, and say yes, it is uncomfortable but we can do it. They really downplay the pain part, most likely to not scare the pregnant girl. They lie, plain and simple.

(The rest of this chapter contains my labor and delivery stories. They are not sugarcoated but aren't horror stories that people like to share—there is even one with *no* pain—but they are the real deal. So, if you are still pregnant, labor is beautiful and amazing. There is no real pain; you can do this. Now skip to the next chapter. You're welcome.)

<u>Baby Number 1</u>

My first baby, we didn't exactly schedule. I had a doctor appointment the day *after* I was due. It just so happened that my doc was on call. The appointment went something like this:

Me: So, Doc, I was due yesterday. When is this baby going to come? 'Cause, you know, I was due yesterday.

Doc:	Well, technically you are correct. I am on call. I can meet you over at the hospital if you are really ready to have this baby. However, due dates are, after all, only an estimate, and we could have any of the dates off.
Me:	Perfect. I am going to go get a bite to eat, and I will meet you over there.

Then I actually did go get something to eat—'cause in case you don't know, once you get to the hospital, they don't let you eat. They claim it is because if you end up in a C-section, they don't want you to puke all over yourself, but again, I am convinced it is just to torture poor pregnant women. They (whoever they are) really get their kicks from it; it is sick and twisted. You are going to expel a human being from your body, and you might need some fuel, but nope, they refuse it.

I was in a lovely little bubble during my dinner. It was a happy time; I was about to have a baby. You get a very euphoric high knowing that you are going to be holding this tiny little bundle that you have been nurturing for the past nine months.

I remember telling my hubby, for the hundredth time, that I did not want any drugs. That the epidural has all kinds of side effects that are horrible for the baby. That it makes their Apgar scores lower and can make the baby not as responsive (and the list goes on and on). That women did this every day for thousands of years without any pain meds and I was just as strong as they were.

My mother once told me, "They have the drugs now, and they didn't back then. That is why they weren't used. If you choose to have the drugs, it is taking advantage of modern medicine. I was going to have the baby in a hospital, after all. By not having the drugs, I would not be a better mother or even get a medal." What did she know? She only had two kids, after all. Me, I knew more than she did, and I knew that I was not, under any circumstances, going to have an epidural.

We got to the hospital, filled out that mountain of paperwork that I talked about, got through all the nurse's questions, and were finally ready to start the show. There was this pretty messy, sticky, weird gel that they put up my woo-hoo. (Drug number 1 for those wanting to start a count.) The first round did nothing. I walked and walked and walked some more. Nothing, nada, not going anywhere.

They did that gel two more times. Nothing, nada, not going anywhere. (Let me tell you, them putting that stuff in is no picnic. It hurt, was weird, and leaked like nothing else.) My options at this point were, first, to start the Pitocin and hope that it would kick-start labor or, second, go home and wait for nature to take its course. Option two was no option in my mind. I had been told that I was going to hold my little girl that day, I had been told that I was going to be done being pregnant. I had been told that I was going to go through this amazing thing called labor, and I was not going home until I did all the things that I had been told that I was going to do.

Finally, the doc ordered the Pitocin (drug number 2). It kicked in quickly. Contractions started almost immediately, and they hurt. They were about five minutes apart, right from the beginning. I was told to walk some more. In my head, I was screaming at the nurses, "You want me to walk?! How the fuck can I walk?!" But I got off the bed and started walking the halls. The more I walked, the more the contractions hurt. My husband, the wonderful man that he is, held the pole that all the drugs were on for me. This way, I wasn't worried about trying to push that thing and maneuver my big belly. I held on to the railing with all my life. Every time I had a contraction, I had to stop. Not knowing what to do, I gripped that railing with all my might. At one point, it hurt so horribly that I was impressed I didn't pull that railing right off the wall.

I made it to the end of the hall, which I was very impressed with myself for doing. Then a particularly hard contraction hit. It actually dropped me to my knees. Have you ever seen a fully pregnant woman down on the ground? No? Know why? Because there is no way to get her back up. Mix that with all the pain and all-encompassing labor, and let's just say it's not pretty. It was at this point that I realized that I had *no idea* what I was doing, that I was in way over my head, and that I'd had no idea, up to this point, what pain was. And there was a very real chance that I was not going to make it back to my bed and was going to have this baby right here in the middle of the hospital, on the floor. It was in this moment that I realized that I had been wrong—oh, so wrong. I wanted—no, I needed—that epidural.

My wonderful husband was somehow able to get me up off the floor, and even back to my room. I told him he had five minutes to find me an anesthesiologist, I wanted that epidural *now!* He didn't even try to argue with me, just kissed my head and told me that he would be back.

Not even two minutes later, he was back, telling me that the anesthesiologist was on break but when he got back, I was going to be his second patient. There was going to be an end to my pain soon.

This was not what I needed to hear. I very calmly (well, at least in my head, it was calm) told him that he now had three and a half minutes to find him for me or not to bother coming back.

To this day, I have no idea how my husband accomplished this feat, but sure enough, he came back, in the time frame that I had given him, with the amazing doc who was going to end my pain. I was floating and pain-free within minutes and was able to spend the rest of my labor sleeping through it. Yup, I was out.

At around 2:00 in the morning, I was woken up by a nurse telling me that it was time. They got all set up and told me that we were going to get started without my doc since the pushing part could last quite a while. I was up for it. I mean, I'd had quite a nice little nap.

They told me to push. Not having any idea what that actually meant, I did what I was told and pushed like I was going to take a poo. I pushed with everything in me. The nurse had the most surprised look on her face. "I can see the head," she told me. At that point, she asked if I could give a little push. And then she told me to stop. Wait! What?!

You want me to what? Stop? That is so not going to happen. Let me tell you, once you start, there is no stopping. Push number two, the head was out, and, thank goodness, my doctor walked in to check on me, since the nurses had not even called her yet. Push number three, and my beautiful daughter was here and I heard her whimpering.

She was perfect: 10 fingers, 10 toes, weighing in at 6 pounds.

Baby Number 2

Let me preface this by saying I was not a nice pregnant woman with this baby. I somehow missed those hormones. Even my poor husband would avoid me most days. There is nothing quite as horrible as a fully pregnant woman on a rampage that has lasted the better part of nine long months. To say it was not pretty is a severe understatement to those who had to put up with me.

I went to my weekly appointment, just like any other week. As soon as my doc entered the room, I demanded to know when she was on call next.

Doc: Well, I am on call today; then I am off for the next three weeks.

Me: Good, then we are going to have a baby today.

Doc: That would be nice, but you are only 38 weeks, so at this time, you will have to wait a bit longer.

Me: Oh, you are too cute, but I am having a baby today. You will either admit me to the hospital and we can do this safely with your help, or I can go home and cut her out myself. Then you can finish delivering her in the ER. Your choice.

I smiled very sweetly and waited for her answer. See, not a very nice pregnant woman.

Doc: You haven't started any signs of labor. Inducing today would be hard on you and the baby. Plus, it could lead to a C-section. It would not be the best choice.

Me (still smiling very sweetly):

	So what I am hearing is that it is not your choice to admit me and evict this baby today.
Doc:	Yes, that is correct. At this time, it would be best to let her cook a little bit longer.
Me (never stopping the sweet smile):	
	Then you have left me no choice. I will see you in the ER when I am bleeding out because I have tried to cut her out myself.
Doc:	Fine, I will put you on the list and they will call you when we have a bed available. I will see you soon.

This is one of my more pleasant stories about being preggo with this girl.

Around 2:15 AM or so, after my fifth call into the hospital, I had a bed. We let my mother know that we were heading to the hospital and that my in-laws would be there in a few hours to take over so she could come to the hospital with me. And off we went.

There was that huge mountain of paperwork that we got to fill out again, then all the nurse's questions *again* before I was finally allowed to get started. But this time, there was a huge difference.

They knew from the last round that the gel stuff did not work, and since I had not started any labor signs, they went straight for the good stuff. My doc immediately ordered the Pitocin. Then the nurse asked me the nicest question in the history of labor and delivery: "What would you like first, the Pitocin or the epidural?"

Let's just say that I signed up for that epidural so fast, I think my husband's jaw fell. The idea that I could have an entire labor free of pain sounded perfect. Until they got ready for that epidural. Let me tell you, that is no walk in the park. Without the pain of a contraction to hide the pain of getting a large needle shoved into your spine, it hurts. And not in the doctor's "Oh, it might be a small pinch" kind of way but in a "Holy cow, my back is on fire and you are trying to shove that needle through me!" kind of way. It is not fun, it is not gentle, and it is certainly not pain-free. With my first, I may have hit on the doc once the epidural was administered. With this one, I just wanted to hit the doc.

But again, I was able to sleep through a good deal of the labor. (Are you noticing a trend here?) To be completely honest, I don't remember a whole lot about this labor. I know it is supposed to be all magical and life-altering, and it is those things. I simply don't remember it. Talk about a bad-mommy moment. All that I remember is this euphoric feeling that I was finally done. I was finally done being pregnant. I was finally done being hormonal. I was finally done being a bitch. There is no other way to put it, I was just happy to be done. If only I had known that this was not the end of my bitchy ways. (Don't worry, you will get to see more of those wonderful bitchy stories coming up in the next few chapters.)

I woke to a nurse in the room telling me that she was going to check me, and asking if that would be okay. Apparently, I was not very nice to the poor nurses. She did her thing and let me know that it was time. She got everything ready and told me to push when I felt like it. Ha-ha. Been there done that, and the last time, I had been told to start, then had to stop. Not going to be doing that again. I demanded that my doctor come in before we got started.

Have you ever tried to demand something from a nurse? Let me let you in on a little secret: They don't like it. In fact, they get a little upset when you imply that you need a doctor. I tried to explain that my last baby had come in three pushes and that the doctor had almost missed it entirely.

Luckily, my doctor happened to be on the floor, heard me arguing with the nurse, and was able to come in to save the poor nurse. Without any further delay, we got the show on the road.

This time, I was able to push the baby out in two pushes. I have to admit, this was my favorite labor and delivery. I slept through the majority of it, had a really short pushing time, and had no pain from start to finish (except for that horrid doctor who tried to kill me by pushing a needle through my back).

We had done it again: another perfect (although unusually hairy) little girl, with 10 fingers and 10 toes, and weighing 7.14 pounds.

Baby Number 3

Oh man, we should have known right from the moment we started to evict this little bundle of joy that she was going to be a handful. All the signs were there that she was going to be her own person. There is no making her yield to my will; she will do what she wants and only what she wants.

It started as any other of my girls' births. We got the phone call around 2:00 in the morning that there was a bed ready and waiting for me. The nurse gave me all of 30 minutes to make it to the hospital, or they would call the next pregnant woman on the list. We quickly grabbed the bag (which, by number three, contained only my toothbrush), kissed our sleeping daughters, and went to the hospital.

It is quite odd that with the first, there was all this excitement, all this pure joy, and I had no idea what I was in for, so the nervous and scared feelings were more on the back burner. By the time that we had our third, those feelings had changed places. I fully knew what I was in for—not just the pain and the process of actually expelling a human from my body, but what came next: the actual taking care of a new baby, my healing body, and two other daughters who needed me. It is a big order, and it is completely overwhelming. Anyone who tells you that each time is full of the same amount of joy is lying to you. With each pregnancy and each passing year, you get more experience, so how can you feel the same way for each labor? Simply, you can't. I felt horrible about this for a long time, guilty that I did not have the same level of joy, the same level of excitement. Let me tell you, it's *okay*. You will still have joy (there is nothing like holding your baby for the first time, seeing your partner hold the baby for the first time, hearing that cry for the first time, or counting all the fingers and toes for the first time) and you will still be excited (What will he or she look like? Will she or he be like his or her siblings?), but it is okay that it is not the same as the first time. But I am getting way ahead of myself. Back to the actual labor.

There was, just like with my other two daughters, a mountain of paperwork, then the nurses asking all the questions that were in that mountain of paperwork, then the waiting around to get the show on the road. By the time we got started, it was close to 4:00 AM. With this one, we actually wanted her to be born on the day we were admitted to the hospital. It happened to be my doc's birthday and was the birthday of a dear friend, so we wanted to push her out that day. We had 20 hours, so it was going to be hard, but not impossible.

We went straight to the Pitocin, and this time, I opted to wait a bit on the epidural. I was a bit more antsy, wanted to be able to walk and move around. Plus, being able to walk would work with gravity to help move her along faster. The nice point about this not being the first time was that I knew what was happening. And with that, I knew when enough was enough. There was no terrified, fully pregnant woman on the floor in a hospital hallway, fully convinced that she was having a baby right there on that floor.

We walked and walked and walked. I walked so many laps, the nurses started counting and cheering every time I lapped their station. They had never seen a woman so intent on walking a baby out of her and were truly on my side. It was empowering to have a team cheering for me when all I wanted to do was lie down and go to sleep.

Even with all the walking and the drugs, my baby girl would not come. The doc advised us that it was time to up the Pitocin drip and see if that would help. Contractions came fast and hard from almost the moment they upped it. It was epidural time, 'cause those contractions were coming every two minutes. When they tell you contractions come every two minutes, that does not mean from the end of one to the start of another. It is from the start of one to the start of another. Then the contractions are a minute and half long. You get only about 30 seconds of less pain before the next one is bound to start.

Once I got the epidural, I started getting hot fast. I was sweating like you can't believe. We had to change my gown at one point because I was soaked, like I had been swimming. My husband had to keep cranking up the air conditioning for me. I could not stand any blankets on me and would complain if anyone was close to me because their body heat was too much for me to handle.

To paint you the picture, there I was, lying in my hospital bed, sweating and beginning to think that I was in a heat lodge. All the while, my poor family (mother, father, sister) was huddled together on the small reclining chair under heated blankets. And my poor hubby was freezing his butt off, trying to take care of me. The room was sitting at around 50 degrees, and I was freezing out everyone else in the room, all while I felt like we were being baked alive.

Then the shaking started. Oh my, the shaking. It felt like I was having a full-body seizure. It was so violent that I could not even talk, my teeth were chattering that much. My frozen room suddenly had lots of movement and my family (all but my husband, 'cause he had seen this before—apparently, I went into shock with my others but I had been asleep so had been unaware of this happening) was in full panic mode. They were trying to cover me up, convinced that I was shaking because it was freezing in the room and because I was soaked again from sweat. They were yelling for a nurse, they were getting heated blankets. It went from being a quiet, serene, frozen state to a full-on emergency in moments.

The nurse came in and told me that it was perfectly normal for women to shake while on a mix of the epidural meds and Pitocin It was nothing to worry about, and though it was not fun, there was no harm to me or the baby. Unfortunately, though, I was going to shake until I was disconnected from the meds. Let me tell you, once the shaking starts, there is no going to sleep. The chattering noise that my teeth made was so loud in my head that sleep was impossible. Luckily, I was almost eight centimeters, so I crossed my fingers that it would not be too much longer.

For those who remember, I wanted her to come on the day that we were admitted. It was now about 10:30 PM. I had only two centimeters to go and a full hour and a half to get there. The doc and I were joking that my little girl was going to be the only baby she got to deliver on her birthday.

We made it to nine centimeters at 11:15 PM, and I started to feel pressure. It was not quite pain, but it was no longer comfortable. My nurse had to step out for her dinner break, and my fill-in nurse told me that it was not pain, just pressure as the baby moved down, no worries. That did not sit well with me. This was not my first rodeo, and I knew that was a load of something. I asked her to look at my epidural 'cause I thought that I was out. Without even looking, she told me that this was not possible, because they plan to give not only enough for labor but for hours after, and even on the very small off chance that it did run out, the drugs would be active in my system for up to two hours after. Again, no worries, you won't be in pain when it's time, she told me. I started to panic.

At 11:50 PM, I was in pain. Not pressure, but pain. We asked everyone to leave at this point and said that we couldn't wait to have them meet our daughter but it was time for us to just be a family. My husband informed the nurse, since between the pain and the shaking, no one could understand what I was saying anymore, that I was in pain and asked that she check me. Her catty response was that she had just checked me ten minutes prior and I was only at nine and a half centimeters, it was not time, and even if I was in pain, it was too late to administer more pain meds. I was beyond livid and started yelling—no real words, just screaming and yelling and screaming.

At midnight, I was saying it was time. My nurse, thank God, was back on shift and came and checked on me. Just like I thought, it was time. My doc came in and jokingly asked if we were going to have this baby in three pushes like my other two. I responded, "The hell with that. I am in pain, this (insert your choice words here) hurts. I am getting her out in one."

The evil nurse was assisting in my delivery and actually had the gall to tell me to stop yelling, that it would not help anything and was very distracting to everyone around us. Well, I had a few choice words for her, at the top of my lungs.

Sure enough, though, I had that baby pushed out in a single push. Yes, a single push, and let me tell you, that was no picnic. It was the first and only time that I had to push a baby out without the help and loving arms of the epidural. It was painful enough that it has seriously scared me from having any more children. Plus with the other two, they cut my woo-hoo, and that tore this time. From birthing the placenta, I swear, I was lit on fire. Those of you women who choose to go through this and then have more kids, my hat is off to you. That was something that I would classify as strange and unusual punishment.

At 12:05 AM (the morning after we wanted her to be born), I heard my third baby cry. Somehow, that little cry (or, as with this one, a very loud wail) made it all worth it. Not that I will be doing that again... *ever*.

Ten fingers, ten toes, 6.3 pounds, and perfect just like her sisters.

My advice to you when it comes to labor: Don't have a plan, and don't have any expectations, because there will always be some part that won't go according to that plan. Now, by all means, make an outline, if that makes you feel better. Do your best to control the items that are the most important. For me, that was making sure that my doctor delivered and that I had my other girls taken care of. For you, it might be other items, and that is okay. Don't beat yourself up if you want that epidural, 'cause let me tell you, it is a miracle drug. Don't beat yourself up if you have a C-section; you still expelled a human being from your body. That makes you a superhero in my book. Don't worry if you have uncompassionate nurses and you yell at them—wait, did I just say that? The point is, you cannot control your labor, and there is absolutely no need to beat yourself up about that or feel that in any way, shape, or form, you should have "done it better." Your story is your story, no matter how it plays out. Be proud of that, mama!

CHAPTER 3

Initiation: The First Six Weeks

I did it. I had expelled a wonderful, beautiful baby from my body. I now had in my arms my precious little bundle. Is motherhood everything I thought it would be and more?

It wasn't everything I thought it would be. There are all these amazing stories about the utopia a new mother enters, how everything in life is now perfect, how you can't go a single minute without looking at your precious baby. How you will watch your baby sleep every moment. While that is all true to some degree, and yes, I had moments of those feelings, I don't want to scare you off. Motherhood is by far the best thing that I have ever done, and I still enjoy watching them sleep (for a moment before falling into bed myself). That is looking at motherhood through very rose-colored glasses.

Our oldest was admitted to the NICU (neonatal intensive care unit, for those of you lucky enough not to need to know what that stands for). When she was about 24 hours old, she started seizing. This was not a full-body, foaming-at-the-mouth seizure like I have seen on TV. This was just a little foot tremble. She was nursing, and looking up at me. Her eyes never rolled back. In fact, she never broke eye contact with me. She never stopped eating. Being a new mom, I really thought that she was just cold, that she was just shivering because her feet were exposed. In one of the many, many books I had read, I had seen that newborns have a hard time regulating their body temperatures. This is what popped into my head as my new baby was having her first seizure. I failed to see it for what it was: a life-threatening condition. Within moments, it stopped, just like it had never happened.

We were prepping to be released, getting me dressed, getting baby girl dressed, everyone happy and excited to be going home when a pediatrician from her doctor's office came in to do a final check and sign the release. She asked how we were all doing. She asked mundane questions about eating, diapers, weight—the normal stuff. I laid my baby on the exam table for the pediatrician to listen to her heart and check her skin, and her poor little foot started shaking again. The pediatrician asked if this had happened before and looked alarmed but calm when I answered that it had happened a few times. "My little girl just likes being all bundled up," I said as a proud mama who already knew her baby. The pediatrician asked if he could move the baby to the nurses' station outside of my room, for them to keep an eye on her. That way, they could see if this was just because of a draft in my room or something more.

That was the last time I saw her for almost 12 hours. Trying to get information was like pulling teeth. No one would tell me where she was, or what exactly was going on. I was frantic and panicked, and that didn't help anything. Luckily, I had a really great nurse who noticed that I was extremely unsettled and retook my blood pressure. With the stress and hormone change, it was high—really, really high. She was able to hold off on my release so I could stay at the hospital with my baby until we all knew what was going on. She hunted down the doctors and nurses to get the information that I needed.

It was from the nurse that we were finally told what was going on. My beautiful daughter was having seizures every fifteen minutes. It was serious, so she had been moved to the NICU and tests were being run. The nurse gave us the news quickly and bluntly. She didn't sugarcoat anything like most of the doctors and nurses there. She didn't talk down to me because I was just a kid, and she didn't hold anything back. She gave it to me like it was, nothing more and nothing less.

My life shattered at that moment. Time stood still; sound didn't enter my ears; I could not process what I had just been told. How could my little girl be so sick? We'd had a perfect pregnancy, she had been watched very closely, I had been extremely careful about what I ate, and all the tests had come back normal. What could I have done differently, and what had I done that caused this? In my mind, this all led back to me failing her. I should have done something differently while I was pregnant. I should have noticed this was more than just her being cold. I should have asked a nurse the first time it happened, instead of trusting my mommy gut.

The nurse led us to where my baby was being tested. I lost it from the viewing area. My tiny pink bundle was being held by a technician while her head was covered in electrodes. There were electrodes on her chest, on her feet. She was attached to a few machines monitoring her every breath, every movement, every thought. There was a lot of beeping as the machines monitored her. The room was lit only by a soft low light and the machines' red lights. My daughter was sleeping peacefully, sucking on a binky. Me? I was anything but peaceful.

My husband was amazing during this; he held it together. He was strong for me when I needed it, and he held me for a long time, letting me cry into his shirt. He let me worry about all the what-ifs that were buzzing around in my head, let me gather myself together and waited for the tears to stop. Then he told me what I needed to hear. He told me: "Right now you need to be strong for our girl. You need to keep it together. You need to be positive and happy. She needs you more than anything right now, and she needs to feel that everything is okay from you." And then we got to go in and see her for the first time since we had gotten the news.

 She looked even smaller then I remember, so helpless, but with my husband by my side and knowing that my little girl needed me to be calm for her, I was able to put on a smile and talk to her. I told her all about her new home, her puppies that were waiting at home for her, how excited everyone was to meet her—anything to fill the silence and drown out the beeping of the machines. She got excited when she heard Daddy in the room. I had to keep reminding her to eat, that she couldn't go play with Daddy quite yet because she needed to eat first.

 We had a neurologist come in to tell us the results of her MRI scan. They had found the cause of her seizures. They put up scans of her brain on the light board and started to explain what we were looking at. Right in the middle of her brain was a bright white spot. He explained that what we were looking at was a part of her brain that had died. It had been deprived of oxygen for a moment at some point, most likely a stroke while I was pregnant. There was no way of knowing for sure if that was what had happened, or any way that they could have detected it while I was pregnant. He tried to tell me that it was not my fault and there was nothing that I could have done differently to prevent this from happening, though I didn't believe him and blamed myself for her condition for many, many years. The only question that my husband and I asked was what this meant for her and her life. And there was no answer for that, other than that time would tell.

For the next ten days, we worked as a family unit to make sure that there was always someone at the hospital for her. We set up a rotation schedule between my husband, his parents, my parents, and me. We had a little meeting about what was to happen while we were with her. There were to be no tears, no stress, just happy, upbeat talking. We were going to make her healthy out of sheer will power. No one was allowed to leave until the next one on the schedule showed up. We would not leave her alone here in the NICU under any circumstance. It was hard, and it was demanding. No one slept, everyone was on edge, and we all had to be happy and positive for her.

After ten days, we got the news that we were dreaming of. She was doing great. There were no signs of jaundice; she was eating well, gaining weight, and making lots of diapers; and most importantly, they had her medications all sorted out and she had been seizure-free for 48 hours. She was able to go home. We were all able to go home.

We got our happy going-home selves into the pickup truck and wedged her car seat in the tiny back seat, in the middle, because that was the only place that could fit her car seat. The car seat was so big that she was partway up by us. I kept telling my husband to drive slower, that the bumps were too big, that she was being jostled around too much. Our six-mile drive home took us forever. My husband and I now laugh that he never got over 15 miles per hour on that drive. We were finally a family, a family that was going home for the first time together.

Walking through those front doors should have perfect. It should have been everything I had been told that it would be. But for us, it wasn't. Our dogs were pissed that we had been gone so long, and at the same time, they were happy that we were finally there. They were curious about what we were bringing home. They were just plain crazy. The chaos that ensued was hilarious as we look back, although at the time, I thought that I was going to go insane from the chaos. Our boxers were 60 pounds and 75 pounds of pure puppy. They were barking, jumping, and licking. Little girl was crying as she was being given her first bath at home, by our male dog's tongue, and as we helplessly tried to get this circus under control.

Luckily, Husband is a quick thinker and had a surefire plan to get this circus to end. He ran into the kitchen, leaving me alone in the chaos, screaming at him to get his ass back in here, begging him to please not leave me alone with everyone. He was able to find a few dog treats and quickly led our dogs out back. Once they realized that they had been tricked, they were not happy. They continued to bark and jump from outside, but at least they were not doing it around the baby and we had some sound protection from the wall.

Those first few weeks, in my opinion, are by far the hardest—not that the tantrums and potty training aren't hard. To me, though, those first six weeks are the most brutal. Not only are you getting used to taking care of a completely and utterly dependent baby and learning about everything that the baby needs to simply survive outside of your body, but you are recovering from a major trauma. Yes, expelling another human being from your body counts as a trauma.

Some of the items that they didn't tell me about is that first poo after having a baby, or the six-week-long worst-ever period that you will be on, or the numbing spray that will become your lady parts' best friend for quite a while. And those crazy pregnancy hormones that you were hoping were going to be gone now that you aren't pregnant—they aren't going anywhere any time soon. Sorry. Yes, you are recovering from a trauma while trying to learn to take care of another person. Remember that you need to take care of yourself, too. When people offer to help, take them up on it.

I didn't take anyone up on their offers to help. I was a very typical overprotective helicopter mommy to my little girl, so utterly convinced that someone would hold her wrong and break her that I would let no one (other than my husband, obviously) hold her. And I mean no one. It certainly made our first Thanksgiving a little challenging.

For Thanksgiving, we packed up everything—and when I say everything, I mean everything: the swing; the bouncy seat, the playpen (or baby jail, as we called it), toys, and the diaper bag full of extra clothes, diapers, binkies (and backup binkies), and changing pads. Then, of course, all the stuff for us: extra clothes, nursing pads, extra bras, even a change of socks. One would have thought that we were going on some big trip, not just to my mother's for a family Thanksgiving dinner. As first-time parents, we just weren't sure what we were actually going to need, so instead of risking forgetting something, we just packed it all up on the off chance that we might need it. Who knew that a little baby would need so much stuff?

When we arrived with our trailer full of the baby's equipment, my mother offered to hold the baby while we unloaded and got all set up. She told us we could put it all anywhere we wanted. This was a kind and simple request to me, though I thought that she was going to break the baby and I pounced into full mama-bear-don't-mess-with-me mode. I was appalled that she would even ask. How could someone who did not know *my* baby possibly be capable of holding her? No, I think not. It was at that moment that I made the announcement, "My daughter is for looking at, not touching. Please do not touch her in any way, and please don't ask to hold her, as I will not be permitting anyone to hold her at this time. Thank you." Yup, I actually stood up on a chair to make that announcement. I even went as far as clinking my glass to get their attention and waiting for them to quiet down.

The response had a few variations: a chuckle, a muffled cough, an open mouth. But one thing was for sure: Everyone thought that I was certifiably crazy. I spent the rest of the evening reminding everyone that baby girl was just to look at, either holding her myself or standing right by whatever contraption she was in at the moment. I was her personal bodyguard; there would be no passing around the baby tonight. To be clear, no one held her until she was close to six months old.

Everyone talks about sleep deprivation and how you are going to need to sleep when the baby sleeps. This was not the case for us. Because of the seizures, baby girl was on some pretty powerful meds, and we gave them to her right before bedtime. From the time that we came home from the hospital, she was sleeping eight-hour stretches at night. I was well rested and recovering well—so well, in fact, I decided to go back to work when she was only a few weeks old. I did not need to recover for the entire six weeks. I was Supermom. But that left the question: What are we going to do with baby? It was not like I was letting people hold her, so day care was out of the question. But I was needed back at the office. One night, my husband came up with what seemed to be the perfect answer: "Why don't we just bring her to the office with us?"

It seemed like the best answer there was. He would be getting much-needed help running the business, I got to be out of the house, and we got to keep baby girl right there with us. He went to work right away setting up an area for baby and me. Over the next few days, he was busy setting up an office for me. When I returned to work, I had an office all to myself, complete with a playpen, a swing, and a bouncy seat all for baby. What could possibly go wrong? This was a great plan and a great setup.

And it was... most of the time.

Within no time, it was quite clear that I could not continue being the main salesperson. It was incredibly difficult to make sales calls with a fussy baby in the background. I would be making cold calls (you know, opening the phonebook and randomly calling all the businesses on the page that I opened to), then there would be a loud cry alerting me that baby girl had woke up and was in need of something. No business owner was taking me seriously with a baby in the background and trying to go out for sales meetings. Ha! There is no taking a newborn to a business meeting. It just wasn't working out the way we had thought it was going to.

The hubby was able to come up with a better plan. He shifted around the people in the office and moved me to office manager and billing with a few sales here and there when needed.

This new arrangement worked much better. I would work mostly on the computer, making sure everyone was billed correctly, and handle all the business's day-to-day stuff. It was very rewarding, being able to work, being with my husband all day every day, working together to grow *our* business, and getting to watch and be with my daughter. Our little family unit had found its groove, and it was smooth sailing.

The nice thing about those first six weeks is that everyone will find a groove. I promise , the chaos that every new mom is feeling and going through will subside. Just breath and "just keep swimming." (You will find out where that quote is from when your little ones are a bit older and you watch Disney movies on repeat for days on end.) It all gets better. You will survive those first six weeks.

CHAPTER 4

Poo
(Because Yes, It Does Deserve Its Own Chapter)

Let's talk about poo. I know it is not a topic that most people would talk about, let alone write an entire chapter about, but once you become a parent, it is surprising how many questions and conversations will be focused around it. Let's be honest—there are only so many things that a baby can do: eat, sleep, and poo.

A word of caution, though: Those of you who are squeamish about the subject might want to skim this chapter or skip it all together. I won't lie; it's not pretty.

Those first few diapers will consist of something called meconium. The pediatrician prepped me for those, saying that the meconium would be devoid of smell, would be of a thick consistency, and would be dark in color. You might think, *Hey that doesn't sound so bad.* Except that the pediatrician completely downplayed what those first diapers would actually be like. While it was correct that they wouldn't have a smell, the rest is just an unreal comparison. Those diapers were filled, and boy do I mean filled, with something that is more like prehistoric tar than anything close to poo that I have ever seen. It will be black and sticky. There is no getting it out of all of those creases and folds without the use of an entire baby wipe container. The dinosaurs had an easier time getting out of their tar pits. Then you will have to somehow wipe this substance off of your baby's behind, back, and private parts. Do whatever you can to keep this stuff off of your hands. A simple misplaced baby wipe, and you will be at the sink trying to scrub this off for a while. Originally I was told that this substance would be in only that first diaper or two. This is wrong. It can last for up to a few days. Invest in lots of baby wipes; you will need them. The only upside to this prehistoric poo is that it clings together. It does not shoot up the back and out of the diaper, or leak down the leg. Silver lining right there.

Then comes the next kind of poo. Again, the pediatrician told me that it was going to be a mustardy yellow, sweet-smelling (if you breastfeed), and seedy. The pediatrician forgot to mention that it is completely liquid and there is no diaper on the planet that can or will contain it. These will happen between three and five times a day. The poo will shoot up the baby's back, will leak down the baby's legs, and will somehow leave the baby's clothing and get all over whatever the baby is on. Swings, car seats, carriers—nothing will be spared. If you are lucky, you will not be holding baby while this happens, or you too will be covered in mustard-yellow baby poo. Just plan to keep extra clothes—for baby, you, and your partner—in the car. Yes, it will always look like you are getting ready for some exciting vacation with the luggage there. Sadly, though, it is just for the inevitable baby poo blowout while you are at the supermarket. Whoever says that it smells sweet is flat-out lying. There is absolutely nothing sweet-smelling about it. My oldest was on an anti-allergy, soy-based formula, and hers smelled worse than anything that my husband could produce.

One night we were having a nice family dinner out, at the kind of place that frowns on you bringing an infant. Because it was Mothers Day, they did not give us too much of a hard time, but we could tell they were not happy to have a four-month-old dining with them. We had just gotten our food, and little girl decided that she too needed something to eat. I pulled out my Hooter Hider (best invention ever, by the way—if you don't have one, I would recommend that you get one ASAP) and started to nurse her. Yup, right there at the table while everyone was enjoying their steaks. Very loudly, she started grunting and kind of fidgeting. Before I had a chance to register what was going on, everything was warm and wet. Yup, she had taken this opportunity to fill her diaper. Little girl was covered: back, front, pants, shirt. You name it, it was covered in yellow poo. She did a number on me as well; my dress was covered, and so was my Hooter Hider. Oh, the smell of it. It was quite unique, really. There are no words to describe this particular stench. But I had forgotten the luggage bag with everyone's clothes. You guessed it: We got to enjoy the rest of our dinner (and dessert) smelling like and covered in bright yellow poo. Lessoned learned: Never go anywhere (and I mean anywhere) without a change of clothes for everyone, no matter how short the trip may be.

My youngest daughter would wait until I was actually changing a wet diaper to take her poos. She thought that it was great fun and oh so funny to shoot that liquid while her diaper was off. When you think about taking a poo, you might think that if you were lying on your back on a changing table, it would sort of dribble out and spread out under you. You would be wrong. It does not dribble out; it sprays out, covering everything that is near your beautiful baby's butt. My youngest would cover the changing table and the floor under it, but as we learned if we changed her near a wall, it too would get the poo spray. I wish that I could say that I was a quick learner and only had to clean it off the wall once or maybe twice. Not me. I never learned this lesson, and my husband would asked me daily, in a totally normal voice as if this is a normal question that every husband has to ask his wife at some point during dinner, "Did you have to clean poo off the wall today, honey?" Ugh, why didn't I just move the changing table?

Once a baby starts solids, the poo will drastically change yet again. It is always a mystery as to what you are going to find in a diaper filled with baby-food poo. It can range from liquid to a complete solid, and from very pale to almost black. All of these forms are considered normal and no need for concern. That doesn't make them any more pleasant or the blowouts any more fun to deal with. To this day, there is a certain shade of orange that always makes me think of diapers.

We went through a period when the *only* foods that one of my daughters would eat were carrots, squash, and sweet potatoes. Can you guess the color and/or consistency of those diapers? I have never been more grossed out changing the diapers of my daughters as I was during that time. Orange, stringy, and more liquid than solid. Saying that they were disgusting would be putting it mildly.

One evening, my husband and I were in dire need of a date night, a grown-up kind of night: dinner, drinks (since I was no longer nursing), and maybe even a movie without cartoons. My mother jumped on the chance to babysit and get some one-on-one time with her granddaughter. We left her with formula and her nightly dinner of carrots and sweet potatoes. And off we went. We came home to find my mother—or more accurately, her shirt—covered in a new orange stain all over her shirt from her hip to higher than her belly button. She had a look of total disdain on her face. My mother, as amazing as she is, is not a fan of poo. There is to be no discussion on the topic, she does not ask about it, and she certainly does not want to be covered in it. She was not at all impressed with the quantity that my little baby was able to produce or the fact that it was neon orange.

I could not hold it in; I laughed hard and long. I may have even snorted. My mother just stood there in front of me in her stained shirt and looking as pissed off as one can get. She found no humor in this whatsoever. When I was finally able to contain myself, all she said was "I am never changing a diaper again," and left. That was the last diaper she changed.

Poo has to be a funny topic; you need to be able to talk about it and smile. You will at some point or another be covered in it, and it is gross. If you don't laugh about it, if you don't keep lighthearted about it, then it will just be a disgusting thing that happens—and something that you need to clean often. Why not turn something that is so gross into something that is just funny, something that makes you smile throughout the day? Trust me, this little shift in your thinking will make your life so much more pleasant.

CHAPTER 5
Breastfeeding

Have you heard the tagline "Breast is best" yet? It was something that was pounded into my head from the moment I announced that I was pregnant with my first, and then every time moving forward when I told someone that I was pregnant. Then there are all those beautiful, idealistic photos of mothers nursing their babies. I knew that I was going to breastfeed. In my mind, there was no question. There was no debate over it. Babies drank the milk from their mommies, end of story.

What they don't tell you is that breastfeeding is hard work. It is not something that comes easily or naturally to everyone. It can be painful, it is time-consuming, there is a learning curve for both baby and you. And despite your best efforts, you might not be able to nurse at all. So, while breast is best, breast is not always in your power to choose. And that is okay.

With my first being in the NICU, my milk supply never fully came in. Even after we left the hospital, I simply could not make enough milk to have her gain enough weight. At her six-week doctor appointment, her pediatrician was concerned about her lack of weight gain and told me that it would be best for my daughter to be put on formula. The doctor used comforting words, that I was able to give my daughter the best start to her life by trying, that I should not feel guilty, and that I was doing what was best for her. But my guilt would not subside. I tried everything that I could think of to increase my supply: extra pumping, special teas, having her nurse longer, but nothing helped. It was completely out of my control. With a heavy heart and full of remorse, I switched her over to formula.

I felt like such a failure, first with her seizures and now not being able to nurse with her, like at every turn, I was just failing her. Although these events were out of my control (as everyone told me), that did not help lessen the guilt. What I didn't realize at the time was that everything was truly out of my control. I was doing the very best for my daughter. So, while the claim is that "breast is best," formula today is a great alternative. There is nothing wrong with making the switch if you can't nurse, or when you are just ready to be done nursing, or if you choose to never nurse. Making the formula choice is not a failure, and you haven't done anything wrong with going that route.

I did not have breastfeeding issues with my other two. Man, they ate like champs right out of the gates. If they were anywhere near my boobs, they expected to be fed, and they ate *a lot*, to the point that if anyone—and I mean anyone—was near my boobs, I was ready to feed.

Showers were particularly hilarious. It didn't matter the time of day, or if I had just fed the baby, once that warm water hit me, I would spray. And not in a fine mist, but like a fire hose. Standing under the water, I could hit the opposite wall in the shower. It would get all steamy, and the glass doors would fog over. I would practice trying to write my name on the doors with the milk spray that I had going on. It is really the only time in our lives as women that we can write our names while standing up and having some body fluid shooting out of us. Men can practice writing their names every time they pee, but we women get only the short time while we supply milk to perfect that particular talent. My ladies would shoot milk from the moment that water hit me to the time that I was able to get out and hold a towel on them. My husband stopped showering with me altogether. He would complain that it wasn't a shower because when he got out, he would be all sticky and covered in milk, then have to shower again to get the milk off.

In fact, if he even looked at me the wrong way, I would spray. For the first time in my life, I had these great big full breasts, and my poor husband could not enjoy them. On one particularly fun evening, the kids were in bed, the house was picked up, and we had energy to burn, which, as new parents, never happened. We crept upstairs, past the girls' rooms, to our room. Just as the fun was getting started, I rolled over on top. And that is where the fun stopped. I unintentionally waterboarded him with milk. He was gagging and yelling about it being in his eyes. He was disturbed on many levels, and incredibly disgusted. Having no way to make it stop, we had to call it a night. He got in the shower to rinse it all off, and I grabbed a pump 'cause why waste it? The night, and romance, was over. Sadly, this was not the only time that our escapades were cut short by the milk spray.

My embarrassing moments aren't exactly limited just to home and the privacy of my wedding bed or my bathroom. They extend to all areas of my life. Once, I was in line at the grocery, on a rare occasion when I got to go by myself. Granted, I was just running for diapers, formula, and nursing pads, but still, I was enjoying getting twenty minutes to myself. I was bouncing around the aisles, not paying too much attention to anything going on around me, fluttering around the store, just doing my thing. When I finally landed in the checkout lane, I started to notice that people were looking at me. They would give me sly little smiles, then look away. I was baffled. The older lady in front of me leaned in and whispered, "Pretty girl, you seem to have sprouted a leak," then looked down at my chest. When I followed her gaze, I was horrified at what I found. I had not only leaked milk through my bra and through my shirt but was actually dripping milk. Ugh, I was humiliated.

I learned my lesson, though. I never went anywhere ever again without a nursing pad. I even went as far as wearing a sports bra if I was able to go out on my own, to help hold them in and prevent milk leakage. For the most part, this solved my problem. But not always. Our business was growing rapidly and doing really great. My husband realized that he had double-booked an appointment one day and asked me if I could please help him out and handle one of them if he had the meetings at the office. No problem, I had worked at the office before with a baby. I could do it again.

Our toddler got dropped off at Grandma and Grandpa's house, and baby girl came with me. I got her all fed and sleepy, and laid her down for a nap in the playpen in my private office. She was out. Everything went smoothly, and my potential clients were waiting in the conference room for me. I got all dressed, smoothed my shirt, made sure my pads were securely in place, put on my professional smile, held my head high, and out I went to meet the potential clients. The pitch went perfectly. They were receptive, and I hit all my points. We even ended the meeting with a signed contract. Go me! Since baby was still sleeping, I went to the restroom to freshen up. Looking back at me in the mirror was not the same person who had gone into the meeting. I had leaked milk around the edges of the nursing pads. Each of my breasts had a perfect wet, milky circle about three inches in diameter. Nice impression I made on the clients there. But they did sign the contract and are still clients today.

On the flip side of the milk-hose boob, you have rock boob. If you never have to experience rock boob, you will be extremely lucky. This happened to me once or twice. I will take spraying milk, stained shirts, and embarrassing wet spots any day over this. One night, I woke up in the middle of the night in incredible pain. The twins were hard as rocks, literally. Knowing that they were too hard for my daughter to be able to latch on, I jumped in a shower. Nothing. It was one time that I needed, more than anything, to dump some milk, and the warm water was not doing its trick. Not even a little leaked out. I pulled out my pump, and it wouldn't attach; again, my boobs were just too hard. There was no give at all for anything to latch to. Crying, I woke my husband, begging him to do anything to get some of this milk out of me. He was groggy and very confused about what I was asking. Once he put two and two together, he told me no way, I was on my own and good luck. I was hysterical, in pain, and not making a whole lot of sense. I just wanted the milk gone, and I didn't really care how. "Just make it stop," I kept telling my husband.

Finally, my body kicked in and started leaking all that milk. It was slow, but it was coming out. I was so amazingly happy to be leaking milk, it was a bit ridiculous. I went from panic, crying, and pain to happy, pure relief and crying with joy in a matter of seconds. "Look, honey, it is coming out; it's coming out," I kept saying over and over.

When it comes to breastfeeding and nursing, you just have to do what is right for you. While I would recommend that you try to nurse because babies get a lot of immune support from their mothers' antibodies that they can't get from formula, it is okay if that is not your choice. This is your baby and your body; only you know what is best for both of you. If you want to breastfeed till your kid is five, go for it. If you want to formula-feed right from the hospital, go for it. A less-stressed mommy feeding formula is way better then a super-stressed mommy who is not producing enough milk because of said stress. Don't let anyone guilt you into breastfeeding if you know that is not the right path for you—'cause let me tell you, people will come out of the woodwork not only to discuss what you are planning on doing with your boobs, but also to offer you advice on what to do with your body parts, and then to even go as far as being upset with you for choosing what to do with your own boobs. It is kind of humorous, if you are able to step back and really listen to what they are saying. Bottom line, though: It is your body, and it is your baby. You are the mommy now and get to have the final say in what goes down. Don't worry, you will find what is best for both of you.

CHAPTER 6
Learning to Speak

There is nothing more exciting then when your baby starts talking. This little blob is turning into a real person, understanding language and able to tell you what it wants in return. For, me this was some of the most fun.

There is nothing like those first words: the joy your child feels when connecting a sound or word to an actual object and then you understanding what that sound or word means. For most kids, those first words come in the form of mama, dada, and cat. My oldest's was ball.

I will remember that day clearly for the rest of my life. She was always a babbler; there was always some sort of chatter coming out of her mouth. We were at the office, and she was over in her childproof (well, it would have been childproof for any other child) area, happily babbling away, playing with her toys. Then it went quiet. Very unusual for my girl. Then I heard "ball" and another "ball," like she was trying it out. Man, the giggles that ensued! She was so pleased with herself for actually saying a word, a real word. She grabbed her ball and ran over to me. Jumping—or, more accurately, hopping—around, she held the ball high and yelled at the top of her lungs, "Ball!"

We were at a grocery store one day—does it seem that a lot of my stories are in the grocery? With five people in this house, we seem to live there.—and one of my daughters had forgotten her bear in the car. The actual shopping had been no big deal, but waiting in line just frustrated her to no end. She started to ask for her bear. I tried to explain that her bear was in the car and we would get it as soon as we were done. Well, explaining waiting to an 18-month-old was not going to happen. She was getting more and more antsy by the moment, as well as louder and louder. When we finally got up to the register, she was yelling, in her adorable toddler accent, "I want me beer. I want more beer. Give me beer," over and over again. People were starting to look oddly at me as my daughter continued to yell about beer. Then their glances moved to what was on the belt, in my purchase. Along with the milk, diapers, and eggs, we had three different kinds of beer. I was convinced that I was going to be stopped while we were leaving and be detained while we waited for CPS to come and sort the situation out.

After that, my daughters seemed to lose their "inside" voices, and everything they said was in yell volume. One evening, we were out to dinner with my in-laws, who are hard of hearing. My in-laws encourage our daughters to yell just so they can hear them. We had ordered my daughter apples to go with her chicken fingers. She was very excited and wanted to tell everyone (the wait staff, her grandparents, the table next to us) how much she loved it. Again in that adorable toddler accent, she proceeded to yell, "I love assholes. Do you like assholes? Why don't you share my asshole? Can we get more assholes?" We tried to explain to her that (1) she didn't need to yell in a restaurant, because we could hear when she spoke in her inside voice and (2) it was *apple*, not asshole. In her head, she was saying it correctly and was very frustrated that we were correcting her speech. Being two and frustrated, she started screaming, "ASSHOLE, ASSHOLE, ASSHOLE!" Nothing quite like being that parent at the restaurant with the toddler yelling obscenities.

It really is a huge milestone when your baby starts talking. To me, it starts the end of the babyhood era and the beginning of toddler time. There is nothing quite as fun and interesting in parenthood as watching that transformation take place. This little bundle of a baby that you have been taking care of is suddenly a full-fledged little person full of his or her own personality and is ready to share that personality with you.

That seems to move us nicely into what happens when you have a toddler who is desperately trying to tell you something and you cannot for the life of you figure out what your child is trying to say.

CHAPTER 7
Temper Tantrums

I wish I could say that my children have never thrown temper tantrums, that I have an amazing secret to share and that with this secret, your child too will never have a temper tantrum, that tantrums are something that only "those other kids" do, never yours or mine, and we could look down our noses at "those moms" who let their kids act that way in public. But the truth is at some point, even the best-behaved kid is going to have a meltdown, and that meltdown might just happen when you are out. And it sucks.

Each of our girls threw a very different type of temper tantrum while we were out in public. We had one who would turn red and fume. That was nice, with no embarrassing kid screaming at us. We had one who would just stare at us with an incredibly creepy gaze, and we could swear she was plotting to murder us while we slept. Then she would turn away, completely ignore anything that we said, and refuse to acknowledge our presence. This was worse than the child fuming because it drew more attention to the issue, and that was what she wanted. But it was nowhere near the embarrassment of having a child just screech at us in that bloodcurdling someone-is-cutting-off-my-arm scream and then just continue to scream until she got what she wanted or we resorted to a public spanking of said screaming child.

Once, we were spending a lovely afternoon at the park with our homeschool group. One of my daughters was very outgoing and was off playing with another few kids in the sand, and my other daughter was sitting quietly with me. She was always an introvert. She loved going to the park, she loved being outside, she loved hearing all the parents talk, and she loved watching the kids play. She just had no desire to actually be involved, and all was fine as long as we left her alone to do her own thing.

Well, there was a new mother to our group who apparently thought that this was completely wrong and approached my daughter. She asked my daughter if she wanted to go play with the other kids. I told the new mother that my daughter was just fine enjoying being at the park, people watching. The mother was very rude about me answering for my child and said that my child's voice was important and needed to be heard. I once again stepped in, letting her know that my daughter didn't like to speak with strangers, thanking her for her concern, and telling her we were good. Finally, this woman got down on my child's level, looked her in the eyes, and told her to go play with the other kids. I was livid, and so was my daughter. Without saying a word, she stared at that woman with the stare that said she was plotting the woman's death, and then she got up, turned around, and buried her face in my legs.

This woman, who was more rude than anything, told me that she dealt with "kids like this" every day and that I needed to have my daughter evaluated, that the sooner we got her diagnosed, the sooner she could begin treatment and the better quality of life she would have when she was an adult. Then she actually handed me her card so I could call to get the ball moving. I took her card, tore it in half, and let her know that my daughter was just fine because she spoke with people, made eye contact, and was extremely empathetic, but just didn't like *her*. I picked my daughter up and walked away. I guess we both threw a little tantrum at the park that day.

Normally, I hold my cool a little better. Although I have no issue holding my ground, I am not usually so in-your-face. I like to model patience and serenity, letting things roll off. But not always. One evening while out at dinner, one of my daughters was fussing. If we are out at dinner, we expect our girls to behave, period. Not just for our dinner, but for everyone else who is paying for a nice dinner. When they start fussing, they are given one warning, and if they do not immediately change their behavior, I take them outside. Normally, this includes a time-out facing the wall until they have settled, and then they must apologize to *everyone* for interrupting their dinners. On this occasion, my daughter was starting to go from fussy to antsy and we warned her that this behavior was not acceptable and if she did not stop right that moment, we would have to take her outside. Then I asked if she could behave or if we needed to go. Miss Sassy Pants said that she needed to go outside. Without missing a beat, we were up and heading to the front door. When we got out there, I scolded her—not too harshly, but she got the point that this was not going to be tolerated, and had her stand in the gravel, facing the restaurant's wall, then I took a few steps back, and turned around. (If I can't see you, then I can't hear you, right? Right.)

Well, an older lady came marching right up to me from out of nowhere and scolded me for disciplining my child. She said I was too harsh with such a young girl (who was well over two at the time) and that she could not believe that I would make my daughter get into the dirt (while still standing on her feet, not like she sat or kneeled in it) and stare at the wall. She was going to get the manager and have him report me for child abuse. Really, for putting my daughter in time-out for acting out in a public restaurant.

She did go get the manager, and she did launch a formal complaint to him about my behavior. The manager thanked her for her concern and turned to me. He then thanked *me* for removing my child and not allowing her to disrupt the other patrons of the restaurant—and for my wonderful parenting, he would like to comp my meal, complete with dessert for the little lady when she was ready to return to her table. *Yeah!*

Well, we all know that children don't always want to eat their dinners before they get dessert. In our house, we don't always get dessert, so on the rare night that we do, it is kind of a big deal, but at Grandpa's house, there is always dessert. One night, we ate dinner, but my daughter refused hers. We reminded her that if she didn't eat dinner, she would get no dessert. She didn't want dinner, so we picked it all up and just a bit later started to dish out dessert. Just like we had told her, she didn't get any. She could still eat her dinner if she wanted, but dessert was out of the question. This led to a full-on meltdown. Man, she went all-out, kicking, screaming, falling on the ground. We called it a night early and started to put our now calm kiddo in the car.

What do you know, but a cop car pulled up behind us and stopped. He got out of the car and informed me that he was responding to a call he received about a young child screaming. Then he asked for my ID. Normally, I would have told him that I didn't have to turn it over unless he had probable cause and that because my child was calm and unharmed, he had none, so he could just shove that request where the sun don't shine, but we had just gotten through a lesson with the girls about how policemen are our friends and protect all of us, that they are the good guys, and that we need to listen to them. Wanting to set a good example for my daughters, who were watching every move I made, I smiled and handed him my ID, with gritted teeth, and got my now very happy and excited daughter out of the car.

She walked right up to him and asked if he was in fact a policeman. He was polite and said he was one. He turned to me and asked me to tell him what had happened. I quickly told him that she hadn't eaten dinner so hadn't got dessert and this had not set well with her. He smiled, one of those smiles that said he got it. He said he too had kids at home who were not happy when they had to eat their veggies before ice cream, and he let us be on our way.

As you can tell, our precious children are not always perfect. There will be bumps, there will be embarrassing moments, and there will be tantrums in public. There is nothing that can be done about it. Even the best-behaved children will push the limits at one point or another. How else are they going to learn that it is not acceptable if they don't do it once (or twice) to see how you react? The next time you see a mother dealing with a tantrum, instead of looking down at her, offer a quick smile and a nod. We all have been there.

CHAPTER 8

The Insanity Starts Again: Adding a Sibling

Life was moving at light speed for us, and before we knew it, our daughter's fourth birthday was fast approaching and we were asking where the time had gone. We had always planned to have our kids two to three years apart, and now our baby was almost four?! What had happened? We had a brief conversation about having another, which was not a discussion at all, more like an agreement that it was now time for another.

We tried, and tried and tried. It seemed like we were trying forever. Then we got the news on the phone from my doctor while I was still at the office, before my missed period. Yup, you read that all correctly. Talk about a memorable way to get the news. It took us a while to let that sink in. My husband actually had me test the next week with a home pregnancy test just in case the doctor was wrong... 'cause you know how often the doctor's office blood test is wrong with this kind of thing.

We told our daughter right away. We made it a big deal for her, took her out, just the three of us, let her know that we had a really big secret for her and that it was just for the three of us for right now. We told her that soon, we would tell everyone else, but for now, it was a happy secret for us. She was over the moon about having a sister. We glanced at each other and had to break it to her that there was a chance that it could be a brother. Nope, no way, not going to happen. She was going to have a sister, and if it was a brother, we could put him back. And that was that.

She absolutely loved watching me grow, and going to all the doctor appointments to hear the baby's heartbeat. She would tell anyone and everyone that she was going to be a big sister and that her little sister would be here soon. We kept mentioning, lightly, that there was a chance that it was going to be a brother and she would love him just as much, but she would still have none of that.

The day finally came. I was 20 weeks along and we could find out the sex. My husband and I talked it over and decided that we needed to find out. That way, if we were having a boy, we had time to get our daughter used to it. My daughter walked right into the ultrasound room and told that tech that there was no need to look, she knew what we were having: a girl. The tech smiled and said she had no doubt that my daughter was right but we were going to have a look just to prove to Mommy and Daddy that she was. Thank the stars, we got the news that we needed to hear: We were pregnant with another little girl. My daughter just beamed; she had been right all along, and now she had proof.

I somehow missed all the really great, fun hormones this time around, making it very difficult for a large pregnant woman to not just be on a rampage all the time. My biggest pet peeve at the time was when strangers would come up and rub my belly, telling me that I was having a boy or a girl. It drove me up a wall. There I was, supposed to be all happy that people were talking to me and interested in the baby. At any other time, a strange woman coming up to you and putting her hands on you, rubbing you, would be considered sexual harassment, but when you are pregnant, you are supposed to be happy about this assault and are supposed to smile, telling her all about your plans for your boobs if you plan on nursing, or that you are having a regular birth by pushing a baby out of your woo-hoo and no, you don't plan on letting the doctor cut your lady parts to make it bigger. While some women would love to have this kind of attention and would love to get to talk to everyone about their pregnancies, for me, it was cruel and unusual punishment. It was simply awful, and I hated it every single time.

One lady came up to me on a particularly bad day, all smiles and bubbly. Man, I just wanted to punch her. Then she not only touched the belly but put one hand on my belly and one on my back, as if that would make it more comfortable. She did all this while asking me when I was due, what I was having, if we were excited, and if I was going to let my husband be in the room when I delivered. This was my chance; I would punch her without her expecting it and would still smile. I looked at her while she was there all bubbling, and babbling about babies and whatnot, carrying on like some crazy woman on a mix of way too many antidepressants and cocktails. When she took a breath, I calmly told her, with a straight face, that I was not pregnant and just carried my weight in my midsection.

Mind you, I was completely pregnant—belly-button-popping-out, about-to-pop pregnant. She went pale and froze, with no idea what to do. I let her stand there in a panicked frozen state for a moment or two before I gently and sweetly asked her to remove her hand from my belly.

I never did let her off the hook and reveal that I was in fact pregnant, due in just a few days, but I would venture to guess that she *never* again assumed a woman pregnant or touched someone without asking. While this may have been a bit mean, I truly think that I did the world a favor by making one less person randomly touch other pregnant women.

(If you skipped over the labor stories that I lumped all together in Chapter 2 so those of you who are still pregnant didn't have to read them if you didn't want to, you can go read the Baby Number 2 story. This labor was the pain-free—or almost pain-free—one, so it is not too traumatic.)

We were excited to show our daughter her new baby sister. When we pulled up to the house, she was there waiting right inside the front door. She was literally bouncing with excitement. Trying to get her to settle down enough to hold her sister took what seemed like ages, but she finally did, and she was thrilled to meet her baby sister. She started talking away to her, just like they were already best friends.

With my first girl, those first six weeks were easy. I bounced right back, slept well, and had a lot of energy, plus there was always someone willing to help out, even though I didn't take them up on it. To be honest, I thought that this one would go the same way. Oh silly me. That precious thought could not have been any further from the truth. This little girl was the exact opposite of my first, and those first six weeks were brutal.

I know, I know, don't compare experiences. Each one is so unique that you should not try to compare; however, we are people, and people like to compare things. Knowing that my only experience was so easy, I fully expected to heal just as quickly and without any uncomfortable moments. As you may have noticed, although I mentioned earlier that you are recovering from trauma in those first six weeks, it was a fleeting mention. That is because with my first, it was not that hard to recover. With this baby, though I had an easy labor, my recovery was much, much harder.

I was so sore that going to the bathroom just to pee was a big event. No toilet paper in the world was soft enough for my delicate lady parts. Even patting was painful. My doctor said that it would be helpful to use a spritz bottle full of warm water. In theory, this is great advice, because you get your woo-hoo all cleaned and if you have stitches, that all gets cleaned much better than if you just pat it dry, all without any TP. Great, sign me up. Except that at that point, you are sitting there on the toilet, all sprayed off and wet. Now what? You certainly don't want to pull up the horrible granny panties with a full adult diaper in them while you are wet. That is just asking for a diaper rash on top of everything else that is going on down there. You can wait to air dry, but who has that kind of time with a toddler and a newborn to look after? Or you are back to patting yourself dry with TP anyway. There is no getting around the TP, or as I called it, cactus paper.

Then you are in pain from washing, and patting. Let me introduce your new best friend for the next few weeks: numbing spray. Oh yes, it is a thing, and it is a marvelous thing, at that. Once you are all done doing your business and drying, you can spray this down there. It is a cold blast from an aerosol can that contains a mild numbing agent, which makes the fact that you are wearing a highly uncomfortable adult diaper with a few stitches (which will get caught on the diaper at some point, so be ready for that) actually bearable. The hospital will give you this miracle spray in your going-home bag.

Get friendly with a nurse and ask for an extra can or two in your bag. You will need it.

And let's just not talk about your poo. That first poo once you are home and off of all the hospital make-you-poo drugs is not pleasant. I thought for sure that I was having another baby and this delivery hurt way more than the first one or that I was actually going to be split in half by the poo. There was nothing that could be done for that pain or burning, but the relief and joy that I felt after I did it, and survived to tell the tale, may have rivaled the joy I felt when I actually gave birth. This only lasts a few poos, so don't worry; you can do this too.

Then there was my baby girl. Until my second daughter was almost a year old, she would not let anyone else hold her. And I mean anyone. Even Daddy could not hold this little girl, or she would scream and scream and scream until Mommy came back and rescued her. We would drop her off at the grandparents' house, walk in the door, and just apologize. We would promise not to be gone for more than an hour, that we would have our phones on us and would return sooner if they needed. They would always smile and assure us that everything would be fine, we should take our time, and everything would be okay. Sure enough, when we pulled back up, we could hear the screaming, the bloodcurdling I-am-being-murdered screaming, from the driveway. She had screamed the entire time that we were away. The moment I took her, she was happy, smiling and cooing and would fall asleep quickly because she had been screaming for an hour. While that is all fine and dandy, it meant that I never got a break. I. Never. Got. A. Break. *Ever.*

Then there was the sleep deprivation. Every mom talks about it. Every mom warns you about it. This was something that I thought that they were greatly overreacting about. With my first, we slept just fine; she slept long stretches right from the get-go. Granted, she was drugged, but she slept. There was no big issue with sleep deprivation. This one, however, I had to put to bed every night. She would go down only while I was nursing or holding her. I would put her down at 6:30, then she would be up at 9:30, 12:00, and 4:00, then be up for the day at 7:00. I could set my watch to it. There was never a night that she slept through one of those feedings. In fact, it was not until she was a year old that she stopped waking up at 9:30. At 18 months, she finally dropped the midnight wake-up call. Then finally at close to two years old, she finally stopped getting up at four AM. Think about not getting a full night's sleep for two years. Even once she was done nursing (around 14 months), she would still wake up, wanting a snuggle with Mommy, and Mommy only, before going back to sleep.

We tried everything that we could think of to get her to sleep through the night on her own. Nothing worked. We tried all different variations of cry-it-out. She would cry so hard that she would puke all over herself and then we got to clean that all up, as well as change the bedding. We tried just opening the door so she knew that I was there, but she would just cry till I held her. There is nothing quite like dealing with a crying child in the middle of the night, all alone, listening to everyone else in the house snore.

There were many nights when the two of us would just sit up and cry together, and no one knew. I would be holding her, crying just as hard as she was, dripping my tears all over her red face, making her that much more pissed off. I felt totally and completely alone in this.

This was a second child, and a challenging one at that, so there were no offers from others to come over and watch the girls so I could get a nap in, no offers to help pick up the house, no offers to keep an eye on things so I could just get a shower in or just pee alone. Plus, I had a toddler to take care of. When the baby slept, I did not have the option to sleep. My other daughter needed attention and one-on-one time. I would have a happy smiling face for her—the one that told the world everything was perfect and this was paradise, during the day. And I would sit up and cry with my daughter at night.

At the six-week mark, my husband was eager for me to "get to work." We had a conversation about all of us working in the office, like we had with our oldest, a big, happy, working family. I think that I laughed so hard when he told me this was his plan that for the first and only time in my life, I had water come out my nose. How in the world could I possibly take both a toddler and a newborn to the office, expect them both to always be on their best behavior and not to make a noise, and have me be functional enough to attend to them while taking care of business? Not going to happen.

After some debate—or rather me stomping my foot that I would not, under any circumstances, be going back to the office—we decided that it would be best for me to work from home. This would give him the help that he needed and would be give me the flexibility to work around the kids' schedules. In theory, this was a great plan. Through rose-colored lenses, we could see absolutely no reason that this would not be the perfect solution. I would work while the kids were napping or after hours when they went to bed. I would be able to work when they were happily (and quietly) playing. Since I was just going to be doing the billing and accounting, there was no phone time and I could just take my laptop everywhere that the kids were. What could possibly go wrong?

Everything could go wrong. Not just one thing, but literally everything. I would constantly forget things that my husband would ask me to do; there was always some payment that wouldn't go out on time; I would be too tired at the end of the day to get any "work" done; the house was always a mess (and boy, do I mean a mess—close to the point of needing a hazmat suit just to enter); kids were unhappy; and there I was, up every night with the baby, in tears about the life I had that was falling apart at the seams.

When talking about working from home, we had decided that my job for the company would entail billing, bookkeeping, and accounts payable. (Mind you, this combination of jobs is a full-time position.) Then, since I was at home, with all my extra time, I would take care of the kids, clean the house, make all the meals, and keep up with laundry and dishes—basically, everything that is related to running a house. (Note that this also is a full-time job.) On top of that, we were homeschooling my oldest, so any and all school-related items (lesson planning, prep work, teaching, and so on) were to be handled by me. (Note: another full-time job.)

No wonder I couldn't keep up. Looking back, I see I had set myself up for failure—or rather, my husband and I set up me up for failure. There was no possible way that any one person could handle that load and stay on top of everything perfectly. There were simply too many balls to juggle to keep them all in the air. But man, at the time, I just felt like a failure—and everything, along with everyone, suffered.

I remember trying to take the girls to the park just to get out of the house. I needed to see the sun, my oldest needed to run and play with other kids, and my baby just needed a change. I was "that mom"—you know, the one who publicly had everything together. My oldest would run over to the playground to play with the other kids, my baby would sit up on the picnic table and play quietly by me, and I would set up a little workstation and get some work done. Looks amazing, right? It should be the poster for work–from–home moms—except really, that was most certainly not how it felt or what was going on in my head.

To me, the chaos would start just with trying to get everyone in the car to go and, more times than not, would end with everyone frustrated, crying, and never actually making it to the park. I would get the baby in the carrier-type car seat (which all my girls rode in until they were two) in the house. Remember, she screamed when anyone else but me would touch her? Well, that did not extend just to people. It meant she screamed any time I was not holding her. To get her strapped into the car seat was like trying to get an octopus strapped into it, without hurting any of those tentacles. Then add a wailing, snotty, hysterical soundtrack to it. And that was how it was getting my loving sweet angel into the car seat.

Once she was in, however, she was great. Actually, she would be get all excited about going in the car. So why the fuss about getting into the car seat? Who knows, but it was a battle every time. Then I would set the house alarm, and at that time, my other daughter would remember she had to do something (like pee) or get something (like a Barbie that would stay in the car while we were actually at the park). We would race around trying to make her happy before the alarm was set. Finally, we would be outside the house. Baby with us and safe in the carseat. Check. The house alarm set. Check. The house locked. Go back to verify. Check. Woo hoo, halfway there!

I would open the car door for my oldest daughter, let her climb in and try to buckle her five-point car seat herself while walking around to the other side to snap the carrier into the base in the backseat of the car, then back around to the other side to check on my oldest, at which time, she would just barely be in the car, and nowhere near buckled. And the arguing would begin. It would go something like this:

"Okay, princess, let me buckle you in so we can go to the park."
"NOOOOOO. MEEEEE DOOOOOO IT!"
"Well, honey, we are going to be late and miss your friends."
"NOOOOOO. MEEEEE DOOOOOO IT!"
"If you want to go to the park, then I am going to buckle you right now."
"NOOOOOO. MEEEEE DOOOOOO IT!"
"Fine, then get out of the car; we are not going."
"Mommy, will you buckle me? I can't wait to see my friends."

This was then followed by her singing happily along to the radio as we drove to the park. By the time we made it to the park, I was already frazzled and fried, but it was time to put on a happy face and make small talk with the other mommies before I could get some work done. We all got out of the car, and immediately, my oldest was running off to play on the swings while I tried to carry the car seat, the laptop bag, the diaper bag, and a drink over to a picnic table. A pack mule carries less stuff than I did. About halfway there, we would be intercepted by a highlighted, manicured mom asking all about something or other, 'cause all that stuff was light and had no weight to hold as she went gabbing on and on about what little Tommy was up to.

Finally, we made it to the park and to the picnic table. Everything was set up: baby in the carrier on the table next to me, complete with her toys, my bags all put down on the ground, my laptop all set up, and last but not least, my don't-mess-with-me bubble up. All of that, and I didn't even spill my drink. How is that for Super-work-from-home Mom?

Sure enough, though, as soon as I was ready to get some billing knocked out or to respond to an e-mail, Meg the manicured mom was back and in my don't-mess-with-me bubble, back to gabbing about Tommy, or my oldest was yelling at me from the swings to look at how high she could go. Or my baby had dropped her toy and was in need of a new one. Then it was time to go home. So much for getting some work done while the kids were at the park. Pack it all in and head home with tired, cranky, and dirty kids, the mom who needed to get some work done defeated and frustrated.

It certainly seemed that having two girls and trying to "work" was getting the better of us. Luckily, with as hard as all of that was, it was not the way life was all the time. Don't get me wrong, it certainly felt like it was that way all the time and it felt like the silver-lining moments were few and far between.
One day, we had a particularly difficult client whom the office staff were just not able to handle. He was rude and wouldn't listen. I got a call on my cell phone from the poor girl trying to take care of this guy. She was just about in tears at how she was being treated, begging me to take the call. What is a woman to do but help out when she is asked? The call was

transferred to my cell, and I rushed with my laptop to the only room that had a lock on the door: the bathroom.

The guy went on and on while I was looking up his account. I tried to explain his account, I tried to be polite while he cursed at me about being overcharged, and I tried to be understanding about his point of view. It was getting me nowhere. I could hear my amazing husband coming home and starting to get the girls riled up. There is nothing more exciting most days than Daddy walking in the front door. I heard him asking, "Where is Mommy?" What he was about to find was something that we still laugh at today.

He opened the bathroom door to see me sitting on the toilet, laptop on my lap, cell phone in one hand, pants down ('cause if you get a moment to use the bathroom, you'd better not pass that up), yelling at a client that he had in fact been incorrectly billed, he had actually been *under*-billed, and if he didn't get off my line right fucking then, I was going to back-bill him for everything that he should have been billed for. And that is how a work-from-home mom does it.

CHAPTER 9
Potty Training

Once you decide to have another, one of the first things that you will think (well, if you are anything like me), *Holy poo; I am going to have two in diapers. Oh no, that is just not going to work. I do enough diapers with just one.* (There is an entire chapter in this book dedicated to the poo of just one child, remember.) *No way, no how am I going to have two in them.* That means you are up for potty training. Hopefully, your kiddo is, too.

Other than those first six weeks, I think potty training is, hands down, the most frustrating part of parenting, for both you and your child. Even the most patient of mothers will cringe and have a story or two about the potty—or better yet, advice on what did not work, 'cause it seems like everyone has a way that did not work. There is no one way to potty train, and the only way that you are going to find what works for you is by trial and error. And that turns into mostly error. Sorry, but that is the fact.

All three of my daughters potty trained differently and at different points. And we tried *every* method known to man to potty train our daughters: going every half hour, using "treats"—a.k.a. bribing—when they went potty on the potty, giving stickers, pleading, begging, reminding. You name it, and we tried it with each child. The truth is *none*—that is right, *none*—of these methods worked for us.

When my first daughter turned two, I immediately started getting those annoying questions from everyone: "Is she potty trained yet?" Yet? As in, she should already be. As if, for some reason, everyone starts to potty train at 18 months. Then there were all of these other moms saying, "Oh yes, my daughter was potty trained in three days," or "Oh, my daughter was completely potty trained by the time she was two," or "Oh, my daughter did it all on her own."

Feeling like I had somehow let my daughter down or was hindering her in some way by not having her at least starting to train, we set out on a mission to have her trained, without any stress, and in a total of three days. Oh, to be a first-time parent and think that this is actually accomplishable.

We were told, as I am sure that you will be told, that when you choose to start this process, you need to make a big deal out of it. There needs to be a mini party, and your little one needs to get all excited so he or she actually wants to use the potty, 'cause let's be honest for a moment: Using a diaper would be so much easier. You can go wherever you want, whenever you want, and you don't have to worry about holding it or knowing long enough in advance to actually tell someone. Then someone else cleans it all up for you while talking and singing to you. Life is much, much easier in a diaper.

Just like all of our good advice told us, we made a big deal about it, talking about it all week while we were at the office, saying things like "You are getting to be a big girl now" or "You are going to use the potty just like Mommy" or the favorite "Are you excited to use the potty like a big girl?" Once the weekend came, she was as excited about something she knew nothing about as she could be. We set off for Wally World to buy the training potty along with the training diapers and all the rest of the training supplies.

Let me tell you, whoever thought that you needed special supplies to potty train was a genius. You know why? Because we spent well over $100 on those crazy things. That's okay, though, because my daughter was ready for this. I mean, she was two, and all. She was all excited, picked a pink potty along with Dora pull-ups, and picked her favorite M&Ms as her treat when she used the potty. What a great plan.

It really was a great day. We got back home from our shopping trip and got everything all set up: the potty in the bathroom next to the big potty, her flushable wipes that she would use to wipe her own butt ('cause they do that right away, and all) on a pretty little side table next to her potty, and a jar full of the M&M's that she would get to have once she peed in the potty. That was where the excitement ended. Once everything was set up, she was so over the whole potty-training thing.

Our daughter loved the pull-ups, but to her, they were just fancy diapers that she got to pick out. We would put her in them in the morning and go sit on the potty. Nothing. But once we gave up, she would get very frustrated that she hadn't gotten an M&M. We already had to adjust the plan—she would get an M&M for sitting on the potty. Well, as you can imagine, this backfired very quickly. She would go and sit on the potty every five minutes, without doing anything, and demand a treat. Okay, we can go with the flow. It is only day one, right? For day one, it is okay for her to get a treat for sitting on the potty. Maybe on day two we will move to only getting one when she actually goes, but for now, as long as she wants to sit on the new potty and stays excited, it is okay.

Day one ended in frustrated tears from all parties. Little girl had way too much sugar, and the crashes were making her very fussy. We ended up going through five pull-ups, and those are not cheap. She was just refusing to go in the actual potty. She would sit on it, then as soon as we would pull up the pull-up, she would pee and ask to be changed. Not a good start.

But I was determined to have a better day two. Day three was Monday and would put us all back in the office. She had to be potty trained, at least during the day, for that. How was I supposed to potty train and work when all I had done on day one was potty train? Put the past behind us, move on to a new day—a day when I just knew it was going to turn around. I was going to stay positive and not let the frustration bleed over; we were going to do this. That was my mantra in the morning, while waking up and getting myself together. I could do this, my little girl could do this, we could do this.

Wrong. Oh, so wrong. Day two went no better than day one. It turns out that days three, four, and five were also no better. By day six, I was pulling my hair out. What was I doing wrong? I was doing everything that the books were telling me to do. I was doing everything my friends with the kids that were potty trained by 18 months and in three days were telling me to do. Nothing was working!

"It must be the pull-ups," one mom mentioned at our park day the following day. "She can't feel when she is wet, so she is not making the connection. You need to go cold turkey and switch her to panties. Then she will potty train much easier." A-ha. That has to be it; if you think about it, a pull-up is nothing more than a fancy diaper, and if she is still in diapers, then how in the world is she supposed to figure out the potty? Got it.

Again making a big deal out of it, back to Wally World we went. We let my daughter pick out the panties that she wanted. She was over the moon about it. So excited. Racing home, we got her in those panties. She pranced around the house, showing them off to everything: the dogs, the plants, her dolls. Proud does not explain her attitude about wearing them. Then she peed, in her panties, on the floor, and was horrified. Screaming ensued—tears, pure panic, about what had just happened. While I was calming her and cleaning the floor, I thought, *Wow, this is great! She won't want to do this again; potty-training drama over.*

We talked and talked about peeing in the potty so she wouldn't get her new panties dirty and wet again. She liked that. We went every half hour. Nothing. But just like with the pull-ups, as soon as we stood up, she peed. While she was no longer panicked about it, she would just stand there and wait for us to clean her (and the floor) up. We tried for days. Days turned to weeks, weeks turned to months. Nothing, there was no progress. She was still not peeing in the potty, and we should have owned stock in cleaning solution. What was wrong with her?

It is simple: There was nothing wrong with her. There was something wrong with me. What I was doing wrong was that I was not listening to my daughter. I was listening to what everyone else was telling me, not focusing on her. This was a huge milestone for *her*. It needed to be done how she needed, when she needed. If your kiddo is not potty trained at two, guess what. That is okay! Take a breath and a step back. It won't be the end of the world, and I promise that when they go off to college, they will know how to use the potty. There is absolutely no need for all the frustration and tears.

So we did the unimaginable: We put her back in diapers and forgot about the potty. We left it in the bathroom, 'cause what else are you going to do with it? But we didn't push, we didn't ask her to use it. Basically, we ignored that evil thing. This let all the frustration around using it go away. We went back to being a happy family. When those moms whose kids were all potty trained would ask, I would tell them that my daughter was not ready and she would let me know when she was. They all thought that I was crazy, that I'd lost my marbles.

As it turns out, on her third birthday while I was changing her diaper from the night before and getting her dressed, she looked up at me and said, "Mommy, today I want to wear panties with my dress." I asked her if she was sure, because we were going to have a lot of people come over and she wouldn't want to get her pretty dress wet. She smiled and said she was sure. You know what, no accidents. She was ready, and that was all she needed.

Knowing this, and being the smart parent that I am, things went differently for daughter number two. We didn't push, we didn't bring it up when she turned two. See, smarter. But all of this thinking that she would tell us when she was ready still backfired.

Once she was about three and half (and we were going to be having another one), I decided that it was time. She was not pleased with this. We all loaded up and went to the store. She pouted. We excitedly looked at all the new training potties. She didn't like any of them. We looked at all of the awesome new panties. She cried. This child wanted nothing—and boy, do I mean nothing—to do with potty training. We picked out all the stuff that I thought she would like, but there was not even a smile from her.

We got everything home, and I tried to be excited about setting it all up for her, showing her all the cool new stuff that she had gotten that was just hers. She was going to be a big sister, and a big girl. Nope, nothing. She was not happy with this. We let it all stay up, hoping that she would wake up and be curious about it. Nope, nothing. Finally, I had enough, and we cold-turkeyed it.

I told my hubby that I needed a week of not going anywhere or doing anything, that our daughter was going to be potty trained by the end of the week, whether she liked it or not. I was not going to have two in diapers. She could pout and head-butt me all she wanted, but enough was enough, and this was going to happen.

It was not the most pleasant week, to say the least. There was no nice mommy about using the potty, and there were no treats. There were tears, and there was lots and lots of pee on the floor. But she hated—and boy, do I mean hated—having pee run down her legs. She learned really fast that if she peed in the potty, it wouldn't do that. By day three, no one was happy, but she was using the potty. On day four, we all were going stir crazy from not leaving the house and everyone was beyond grumpy. On day five, though, we saw the light. There were no accidents, there was no pee on the floor, and my daughter no longer had to be reminded to pee or to be asked if she had to. And on day six, we all left the house. We did our first outing sans diapers.

Does sheer force work to make a child potty train? While it did work for us, for this child, I would certainly not recommend it. It was not fun, and I think I cried more than she did. And the frustration was over the top. It did not help that I was pregnant and had a girl I was trying to homeschool, all while trying to potty train. It was not, in any way, a pleasant experience for anyone involved. We wouldn't be trying that way again.

So what does work? It seems like treats, bribes, stickers, repeatedly going to the potty, and sheer willpower all seem to fall a bit short. Yes, both the girls got potty trained, but neither of them had a positive time with it. With my third one, I was back to square one when she had to be potty trained. I had no idea what to do, was out of ideas, and certainly did not want to go through all the tears that we had with the other two. I was on the hunt for a method that would work, that would be easier for everyone involved.

Then it hit me: What if we take this super-slow with teeny, tiny baby steps? I felt like a genius. Why hadn't anyone else thought of this, I wondered. I planned to start once she was two and a half. It was right around this time that she started to notice that her sisters didn't wear diapers and that they used the potty. She asked all kinds of questions about the potty and how to use it and why we used it. Me being the brilliant mommy that I am pounced on this time. We bought her own little potty and panties, and we got home and set everything up for her. Then we made her wait. We told her that this was all for big girls and that when she was three, she would be a big girl, that they didn't make diapers for three-year-olds. A little reverse psychology never hurt anyone.

She looked at that stuff every day and would ask if she was three yet to use it. Finally, her birthday came. I think she was the most excited about being able to use that little potty. She proudly woke me up, saying, "Mommy, it's my birthday and I am three. I want to wear panties and use my potty. I am a big girl." And so we did. We put her right into the panties. She was determined to use the potty, her enthusiasm was high, and she was happy and excited. Sadly, it did not go as smoothly as we had hoped. She was able to make it some of the time while we were at home, if she was reminded and nagged, but not often, and if we were out, forget about it. She would be way too interested in whatever we were doing to remember that she had to pee, or too engaged to be pulled away to just use the potty.

Since I had made such a big deal about using the potty and her being a big girl, there was no talk of putting her back in diapers. She would not hear of such a thing. While she would wear a pull-up at night, there was nothing to wear during the day but a pair of My Little Pony panties. Ugh.

My poor little girl was heartbroken. She so wanted to be a big girl and use the potty just like everyone else, but she simply could not figure it all out. She would feel she had to go and would race to the potty just in time to pee all down her legs right next to the potty. Screaming would follow. She would be so upset that she couldn't actually say any real words, just give a high-pitched wail. The poor baby was very frustrated and upset that she was not getting this. While I wish I could say that I was a perfect example of patience and that this didn't rattle me at all, that would be a lie, and anyone who says that potty training won't rattle them at some point will also be lying or idealistic. I may have lost my cool once or twice with this.

But then my in-laws became ill and needed me to take care of them. There was no way that I was going to make some teenage babysitter deal with a frustrated, cranky three-year-old. After some persuading, my daughter agreed that she would take a little break and would wear diapers again. She made sure that she was still a big girl and had me tell her many, many times that she still was one. I think that she was actually relieved with this, to be back in diapers and taking a small but well-needed break from the potty.

My husband and I spent the next few months taking care of his parents, while my daughters spent most of their time with a rotation of different sitters and family members. And finally, we were starting to get back to normal. Time to get back to potty training.

Nope, no go. She wanted nothing to do with using the potty again. There was not a bribe on the planet that she was willing to take to try that whole potty thing again. All I can say is if you have a stubborn kiddo that is refusing the potty, good luck. It is hard work to go from a bad potty experience back to diapers and then back to the potty.

With luck and a little bit of patience, one day your little one will be ready to tackle this problem again. For us, I would simply ask her every morning, when she was getting dressed, "Would you like a diaper or panties?" and it would be her choice. There would be no begging on my part to *"Please* figure out this whole potty business," and there would be no drama on her side about not wanting to wear panties. She simply picked the ones that she wanted.

For quite a while, I would swear that she would always choose a diaper, but I never asked again or tried to tempt her choice. There was no guilt about a diaper, and no pressure to wear panties. All was in her control. Lo and behold, one day she said she wanted to wear her My Little Pony panties again. Without any celebration or attention to it, I just put her in the panties. Secretly inside, I was jumping for joy and happy for her. She was ready to try again.

This time went much better. While there were still accidents, they were nowhere near as frequent as they had been. She had just about mastered daytime potty training (Why try to potty train during the day and ask them to try to stay dry at night all at once? Remember, teeny, tiny baby steps—keys to success right there, I tell ya.) when we had a move. We were moving, the kids were going to be getting new rooms, sleeping in new beds, lots of changes.

Back to square two. Yup, you read that right: square two. Diapers were square one, and she flat-out refused to go back to wearing diapers. She was determined to figure this whole thing out. She was going to use the potty. Square two: she was wearing panties but back to peeing on the floor right in front of the potty. Not a good place to be in a brand-new house with brand-new flooring. I was baffled. She had been doing so, so, so well, and this was a major step backward. And don't even get me started on nighttime. Although she was in pull-ups, she was back to waking up wet every morning. Having to deal with a major life-changing event (or two) during potty training is not fun and is beyond frustrating.

After a few days, which felt like months, she was back in the go. Woo hoo, win!

My advice for parents who are potty training, will be potty training, or are pretending that their kiddos will magically self-train: Don't listen to what *anyone* else has to say. Don't listen to the advice on how to potty train, don't listen to Debby the manicured mom who says that her Tommy was completely potty trained by 18 months and in three days. Listen to your child, go by your gut. You will always know what is best for your child, and the best way to go about it. Try to tune out all the other voices talking to you. And be prepared to drink a lot of wine, so stock up at the store.

CHAPTER 10

Let the Rivalry Begin

Once my baby turned into a toddler, things started to get hard. As if working from home with two little girls was not hard enough, now I had a toddler who refused to nap. While this seems like a little thing—I mean, babies turn into toddlers, and toddlers give up their naps at some point—it started a downhill roll for us.

Without my toddler getting an afternoon nap in, my oldest was not getting her precious one-on-one alone time in the afternoon. This left her fussy and looking for ways to get that undivided attention, which had my normally very well-behaved daughter acting out. Then when I shifted to give her some attention or redirect her, my toddler would get into something.

Oh, let that sibling rivalry begin. They would compete about everything, whether they were actually conscious about it or not. They would fight over what toys they played with, what book we were going to read, and who got to play with the dogs. They would fight over who got to wear which hair bow. You name it, and it was a fight.

For me, this was understandable. I grew up with a sister and understood that all these little items would have us figure out the pecking order in the family and that each item was to be treated like it was the end of the world. If one child gave at all, the other could exploit that and the child who gave would be lower on the totem pole, so everything was a big deal. But to my husband, who grew up as an only child, this was weird and twisted behavior. He just could not get his head around why everything had to be a fight and why sharing was such a big deal.

He would come home and the girls would be going back and forth about some toy. Truth be told, it wouldn't even be a toy that either of them liked. They just didn't want the other one to have it. He would get involved and attempt to mediate. He would do his best to figure out what was going on and to try to come up with some solution that both kids would be happy with. Then he would be flabbergasted when both girls would end up in tears and neither of them would be happy. There was no way to make them both happy.

He would come to me in complete disbelief that he couldn't work this out. He could mediate complicated business situations. He could have large groups of people come together on all kinds of ideas. He was a master of the win-win compromise, but when it came to these girls and a Barbie, he could not for the life of him figure out the elusive win-win. I told him there was a secret.

There was one simple phrase that would make them stop whining. It would make them stop fighting. It would have them come up with their own win-win situation. But it was to be used with discretion and not at every chance. Since it was a powerful magical phrase, we didn't want to wear it out. His eyes were wide. He could not wait for me to reveal this all-powerful magical knowledge.

Figure it out.

Three little words. Isn't it odd how some of the most powerful phrases we say contain only three words? Figure it out. That was it. When they would get into it and the whining and fighting would get to be too much for me, I would simply yell out, from wherever I was in the house, "Girls, figure it out." This would get their attention. It was a call that said, "Get your shit together, 'cause Mom is about to lose hers." It caught their attention, and they (even as a preschooler and a toddler) would be able to work out a custody agreement with the toy in question really, really quickly.

Now, there were a few occasions when this magic wand didn't work. I mean, they were kids, after all; they had to test that boundary to find out if it really held the same power as it had the last time they had tried to push it. Once, my daughters were fighting over a baby doll. Mind you, we had hundreds of baby dolls. (No, I am not exaggerating, literally hundreds.) I called out, "Girls, figure it out." Nothing happened. It was like they hadn't even heard me. They didn't try to figure it out, they didn't stop whining, and they certainly didn't come up with a win-win solution.

Off I went to the girls' room and calmly asked them what was going on. The hysteria that ensued was comical. Both of them were red-faced, with tears streaming down, trying to talk over each other. They both wanted to be the mommy, they both had been playing with the baby first, and the other one had taken it away. You could almost think that they had been seriously wronged. I had to shout to be heard over them: "Enough!" I gave them a moment to settle down and catch their breaths. I gently took the baby doll out of their hands, since they were both holding on to it—one holding an arm, the other holding a leg. I took the baby doll into the kitchen, where I put her on top of the fridge, then I turned around and went back to cleaning the living room.

My girls, for the first and only time in their lives, were speechless. When they finally had a chance to process what had just happened, they asked me who got to play with the doll. I told them that I had come up with a solution: Since they were not able to play nicely together, then no one got to play with the doll. They learned really fast that they did not like when Mommy had to get involved. It took me getting involved only a few times for that phrase, "figure it out," to really gain traction and stick. I think that doll stayed on our fridge for the better part of a year as a nice reminder of what happens when Mommy has to get involved.

These three little words certainly carried weight, even as the girls got bigger. My favorite was when they would be fighting over what to watch on TV. In our house, the TV stayed off most of the time. When we turned it on, it was a big deal, but when they got to pick what to watch, it was a huge, best-part-of-the-day type of deal. With more than four years between them, however, trying to find something that everyone would like and that would be appropriate for everyone was a bit of a challenge. They would go back and forth; one would want something from Disney, the other would want cartoons. Back and forth it would go. I no longer had to yell those words, just tell them quietly to figure it out. They would magically agree on something else. Maybe it would be a princess movie. Maybe one would just give in so I wouldn't turn off the TV. Maybe they would choose to take turns. In any case, they would peacefully figure it out.

Even now as they are no longer toddler and preschooler, they are able to find a compromise with each other on all types of issues. We were lucky that by the time my daughters were seven and three, they had figured out how to handle most issues without too much of a fight. They were each other's best friends, worst enemies, and biggest cheerleaders.

Find a phrase that works for your family. It needs to be short and sweet, something that you don't have to yell at them, but something that you can say in a calm, gentle voice, that will get the message across that they need to adjust their behavior or you will be getting involved. Then if they push, you need to get involved and remove whatever they are fighting over. The key to this method is being able to do it all (say the phrase and follow through) without any emotion, without having your feathers ruffled. That is the real power: Your kids will be shocked at your lack of involvement. If you need a Mommy time-out (you know, when you are hiding in the bathroom, alone, with the door locked) before interfering, that is just fine. Get your time-out in, cool down, then do it. The kids don't need to know that you needed a breather before going in there.

Another item that was helpful in resolving the rivalry was being able to spend one-on-one time with each girl. Giving each her own alone time was simple: We would just plan for Daddy to take one and I would take the other. Then the next time, we would switch. It was easy for us to divide them up; each would get a parent's full attention when she needed it.

One-on-one time is very important. It shows your kiddos that although they are important together and when doing things as a family unit, they are also important alone and that having check-in time with them is important to you, that you are interested in what is going on with them. Each girl got to pick what we were going to do, without having to be worried about what her sister would be interested in doing or if it was appropriate for them to do. They had a few times a month when time was just about them. Plus, what is better than a date without any fighting or whining, and it was always fun to find out what they wanted to talk about.

We seemed to have found a groove, and it was smooth sailing.

For about all of a moment.

CHAPTER 11

Insanity All Over: Adding a Third to the Mix

One day, it dawned on me that my husband and I were about to be 30. I was in panic mode. We had always said that once we hit 30, we were going to be done having kids—whether we had one child or six, we were done at 30. Not that 30 is too old to have kids, but he had grown up with older parents, and it was important to him to be closer in age to his kids. Plus, I had always envisioned my midlife time as full of traveling and doing the things that we wanted as a married couple. That is hard if you have a toddler or even a teenager running around.

With this end date coming fast and my clock ticking, the idea of never holding a baby again, never holding my baby for the first time, never hearing first words again, the idea of ending that whole chapter in our lives was sad. I was not ready to be done, to have something so final. I told my husband that I wanted another baby. Even with as hard as my previous one had been, I was not done. He asked if I was really sure and said that he was on board with whatever I wanted but that I needed to be really, really sure that I wanted another one. Without missing a beat, I told him I was.

Then I started to rethink this. Did I really want to have all those sleepless nights again? Did I really want to go back to changing diapers? Go through potty training again? We were finally starting to have a life again; the girls were old enough to leave with a sitter. There was no nursing, so I could have a drink (or two) if I wanted. Shoot, the girls were big enough to take to a movie theater for a fun evening out. Plus, with my youngest getting some more independence, I was able to actually get some work done. The days of failure and nights of tears were all behind me. Did I really want to go back to those days?

Oh no! Second thoughts and doubts were creeping in.

Well, for the first time ever, we got pregnant the very first month that I was off the pill. The universe decided for us and said that we were destined to have another beautiful baby. I was thrilled and terrified all at the same time. My husband would ask if he was going to get the happy pregnant lady who loved life and was a joy to be around or the bitchy on-a-rampage lady whom he was going to hide from for the next nine months. I bet that you can guess the type of answer he got.

Like with the other girls, we wanted to keep the pregnancy a secret, but by nine weeks, I was wearing maternity clothes and showing. There was no keeping this a secret. I was already huge. They say that you show earlier with each pregnancy, and this was true for me. We had to tell people; otherwise, they were just going to think that I was gaining a ton of weight for no good reason. I was *huge* already, like couldn't-wear-my-wedding-rings-by-week-12 huge.

For the first time, the news was received with mixed reviews. With our first and even our second, everyone had been thrilled. Everyone had congratulated us. This time, though, people would laugh and ask why. Or they would mutter something about having a large family in this day and age. It was not what we had been expecting, to say the least. My husband says that I was just oversensitive and that I was reading more into their comments than they really meant. But when you're pregnant, any time that *anyone* laughs at you, you are going to take it to heart. It is just not nice. So, word of advice: Don't laugh at pregnant women.

I was at the store with the two big girls and my big belly. The girls were being good but loud, and frankly, I was too tired to correct their behavior or ask them, again, to use their inside voices. We went to check out, and the cashier looked at my girls, looked at my belly, and then, with a smirk, asked me if I knew where babies come from. I stared at her, completely in shock that someone would actually ask another adult they didn't know if they knew where babies come from. Then she asked a follow-up question: "I mean, do you know how they get in your belly?"

Wait, what?

I stood there with my mouth ajar for a good moment or two. It took me quite a while to process what had just come out of her mouth. Then it hit me what had just happened. I found my voice and the perfect response. "No, I don't. I just keep getting pregnant. Please tell me that you know how and could please let me know what I keep doing." My response left her with her mouth ajar. I gathered my things, and we all left.

People would take a look at my two girls and ask me if I was hoping for a boy this time. I would always smile and reply, "As long as the baby is healthy, I am happy." This was a lie. Yes, I wanted a happy, healthy baby, but that was not all that I wanted. I wanted another girl. In fact, I was terrified that I was going to have a baby boy. While I have no doubt that I would have adjusted and would have figured out what to do with boy parts, I did not want to, and that is horrible to say. But it is the truth. I knew girls, I had all the girl stuff, and we enjoyed doing all the girl things when Daddy was away at work. It was going to be easy to slide another girl into this picture. But a boy? A boy would disrupt everything—but you just aren't allowed to say that.

With my first, I knew it was a boy. They always say that a mother's intuition is spot-on, that a mother knows what she is having long before an ultrasound can tell you. I knew I was having a boy. When we got that first ultrasound and the tech told us it was a girl, I didn't believe her. In fact, I may have gone as far as to tell her that she needed to either go back to school or pick a new career because she was flat-out wrong. I then had them check at every ultrasound we went to, and I continued to tell every tech that he or she was wrong, because I was going to have a boy.

And I had a beautiful girl. Silly me.

With my second, I knew it was a boy. Although I wasn't as rude to the techs this go-around, since I had been so wrong the first time, I wasn't entirely sure they were right. I hoped they were right, I told the universe we needed another girl because my daughter was having nothing to do with a brother, but secretly, I thought that I was having a boy. Thank goodness I was wrong. So far, that mother's-intuition thing that they talk about was just crap, 'cause my intuition had been batting zero.

With this one, I knew it was a girl—and that terrified me. Knowing my history of being so wrong when I was so sure about what I was having, I felt horrible for being so anti-boy, so I didn't tell anyone. I kept it to myself that I thought I was having a girl, which must mean I was actually having a boy and that I was not happy about this. When we had our second, we had to prep our oldest daughter that it could be a boy and that there was a possibility that she could have a brother. This time, I had to prep myself.

"I could have a boy. I would be okay with a boy. I could be a baseball mom. It would be fun having a son."

These were all the things that I would tell myself. I knew they were lies; I knew that I never wanted a boy. But it is a 50/50 chance, right? At some point, we had to roll a boy. I spent the first 18 weeks of this pregnancy stressed and sick over those odds. Sure, people blamed morning sickness, but I knew the truth. I was so nervous about having a boy that I was literally making myself sick over it.

Doomsday came, and it was time to find out the sex of the baby. Everyone was so excited at my house. The girls were having a debate with Daddy about the benefits of having another sister over having a new brother. They were going into great detail about why they needed another sister, and my husband was having nothing to do with it, having all of his own reasons for needing another guy in the house. They were giggling and laughing, they were making bets, they were having so much fun. Me? I was a scared, sick little (or rather huge) ball of pathetic.

We walked into the room. Luckily, it was a new tech, not one of the ones I had traumatized throughout the past couple of pregnancies. She was all kinds of bouncing, bubbly, happy personality, asking the girls if they were excited to find out if it was a brother or a sister. My girls told her there was no need to look; it was a girl. She turned and asked my husband if he was praying for a boy. He laughed and said he could only hope. Then she finally looked at me and asked if we wanted to know. All I could do was nod.

She made all the normal checks. Everything was looking normal, for the most part. We had a few little things come up that she was going to have to have the doctor come in and talk to us about, but other than that, everything was good. Then it was time. She poked, and squished, and pressed. The baby was not in the best position to get a good look. She said we had a few options. We could wait a moment to see if the baby would change positions, she could make a guess based on what she could see, or we could wait and see at the next appointment. I didn't want a guess. I needed to know and couldn't wait for the next time; I was too stressed for that. The tears were welling up in my eyes. This was not what I needed, I just needed to have my fears confirmed. A boy. I knew it was a boy.

Just then, baby rolled completely over and gave us a good show. The tech smiled and said, "Well, girls, I hope you made a good bet. You're having another sister."

My tears started flowing. "Are you sure?" I asked her. She patted my shoulder and said she was 100% sure. There was no way that this could possibly be a boy. The relief that swept over me was amazing. For the first time in the pregnancy, I started to be happy and excited.

As I got bigger, the excitement continued to get bigger, right along with my belly. My mornings would start with the girls talking to my belly. They would often whisper to it. When I asked what they were saying, they would look up at me with smiles, responding, "Just sister secrets, Mom. You don't need to know," or "Mom, we aren't talking to you." They would ask every day if today was the day that we were going to bring her home.

My girls couldn't wait for this baby to come out. With my oldest being eight and having been through this before, she knew what to expect. She couldn't wait to hold the little baby, or help take care of her, but the other daughter, being only three, thought that I would be having a toddler just like her. She was convinced that I would bring home a playmate for her and that she would spend hours setting up her toys just right so they could play together. The whole idea of a baby was beyond her. She could not wrap her head around the fact that the baby wouldn't "play" for quite some time and that for a long time, all the baby would do was eat, sleep, and poo.

The day (or should I say night, since it was two in the morning? Evil, evil hospital staff...) came, and my husband and I left for the hospital to have our baby girl.

(I lumped all my labor stories together. If you have not read them because you are still pregnant, I would not recommend reading this one. None of my stories are horror stories or anything that bad, but this was my hardest of them all. There may have been yelling and cursing involved. You have been warned).

We had the baby just after midnight, and I was exhausted. We let all the family in to ooh and ahh over her. By the time everyone left, it was close to two AM and my little baby girl was not ready for the party to be over. I called in a nurse and asked if she would mind taking my daughter to the nursery so I could get two hours of sleep. If the baby needed fed before then, they could bring her back, but I really needed some rest.

This completely horrified the nurse, to the point that she physically took a small step back, like I was going to hit her, and told me that the hospital I was at no longer had a nursery for healthy babies, and they did only room-ins so mother and baby could bond and the hospital did not have to separate them. Studies have shown that this was best for both mother and baby, she said. That was that, and she walked out—well, really, she hostilely walked out. That nurse and I never did get along.

Way before I was ready that morning, I had a knock on my door. In ran my other daughters. They came running in, ready to see their sister. My husband was trying his best to keep them from being too loud, in case either I or the baby was sleeping, and trying to keep them from being too crazy. It really was a sight to be seen.

My oldest ran right to the side of my bed and got up on her tippy toes to see over the bumper, her face full of curiosity and excitement. "Where is baby sister?" she asked, absolutely no patience to wait one second longer. I told her that the baby was lying there with me and that if she could be gentle, she could climb up to see.

Without missing a beat, she was up on my bed with me, looking down at the new little baby all wrapped up in a pink blankey. "Can I hold her?" she tentatively asked me.

"Of course. You are her big sister; you can always hold her." Now keep in mind, if this had been my first child and another kiddo wanting to hold her, I may have had a panic attack. By baby number three, I was a bit more relaxed. I realized it takes a whole lot to break a baby. In fact, with baby three, everyone who visited me in the hospital was able to hold her, even walk around while holding her. Quite a difference from the first baby.

My oldest daughter was overjoyed to be holding her sister. My middle one was still clinging to Daddy's leg in the doorway.

"Princess, would you like to come and see your sister?" I asked, looking over at her. Slowly, ever so slowly, she crept over to the side of the bed. I will never forget the look on her face when she saw her baby sister for the very first time. Her eyes went big, and her mouth dropped open. She was in complete shock at what she was seeing. That little pink bundle was not at all what she had been thinking would be coming home with us. She was not thrilled about this little bundled blob. She still climbed up on my hospital bed and asked to hold her sister, but she was very unsure.

She had been expecting a new playmate, someone she could pal around with—a walking, talking, full-fledged kid just like her—but what she was holding in her arms was something on the other end of what she had been thinking. And she was not pleased.

"Mommy, what is this?" she nervously asked me.

"Well, princess, this is your new little sister," I said while trying to keep a straight face.

"This is not what I was wanting. I thought she would be able to do *something*," she whined.

"Don't worry. One day, she will be able to run and jump and play with you. She has to grow a bit before she can do all of that, but right now, she is still a little baby." I tried not to laugh at her face while she held her sister and wanted—no, demanded—to play with "it."

I was ready to go home. Now, I know the policy is for new moms to stay at the hospital for 48 hours after birth and as long as there are no complications, they can be released after that. The time starts after you deliver and are all settled into your recovery room—at least that was how it was for my hospital. By the time that all my family and friends had left our delivery room (the nurses were okay with us chilling in there since it was a slow night), it had been close to two AM. Then we had gotten all moved, which is no picnic, and by the time the new nurses in the recovery ward had me officially checked in, it had been close to three AM. My daughters were there promptly at eight AM. I still think that Daddy had them in the waiting room long before then, just waiting for eight AM to hit so they could come in, and I was ready to jet. There was no way that I was going to be staying here for another 43 hours. Nope, not going to happen. Let me go home, now.

My nurses were very polite and nice, although they treated me like this was my first baby. I knew me, I knew my family, and best of all, I knew that they had no nursery for my little baby to go to so I could rest. If I was not going to be resting here, then I wanted—no, needed—to go home. This was not my first rodeo. I knew what to look for, I knew what was normal and what was not, and better yet, I knew what was normal or not normal for my baby too.

Don't worry, you too, will have all those maternal instincts down, and better yet, they will be spot-on. Sure, you will have a hiccup now and then. I mean, we (moms) are not perfect, and there is no such thing as Supermom, but for the most part, you will know when to call the doc, when to wait it out, and when to just head to the ER. You will have learned from trial and error or, if you are like me, mostly error. But those days will start being behind you with every child. Don't be afraid to push for what *you* think is best for you and your child. Yes, the doctors (and nurses) have gone to medical school and know a whole lot more than you when it comes to most things medically related. Don't dismiss their word altogether, but on some of the other points, trust your gut and get it done.

My doctor came in to check on me, and I told her that I was ready to go home. Luckily, I had the same doctor for all three pregnancies and all three labors. She had seen me at my best, and she had seen me ready to give myself a C-section to get the baby out. Better yet, she knew that I knew myself and that I had no issue with calling and asking her nursing staff questions if I thought something was wrong. And she gave me the okay to recover at home, as long as I could talk the pediatrician into letting baby girl go home too.

That was a whole lot harder. The pediatrician's office sent a different doctor every day, so the doctor that we'd had the night before was not going to be the doctor that we were getting today, and the chances of actually getting the girls' pediatrician was 1 in 26. Yes, there are 26 doctors at the office my kids go to. It is great going to a big office, because we can get in the same day, no matter the reason. We can get the kids all scheduled at the same time so we are in and out quickly. There is always a nurse who needs something to do to answer all kinds of random questions. But when trying to jail-break out of the hospital early, it is not such a great thing, because chances are that the person who is coming in is one you have never seen before.

That was certainly the case with us. A new male doctor came in and introduced himself to me. He was a bit surprised to see baby girl and me all dressed, the room all packed up, and a car seat all ready to take her home. He looked over his paperwork again.

"Miss, it says here that you were only admitted to this ward at three this morning," he stated, but his statement sounded more like a question than a statement, like somehow he had been given the wrong information on the chart or a nurse had written the time wrong.

"That is correct. And we are ready to home. My doctor has already signed off on it and sent in all the paperwork. All we need now is for you to take a good look at baby girl here and sign her papers. Then we will be on our way," I said as brightly and cheerfully as possible, since it had not yet been 12 hours since I had expelled a human being from my body—quite painfully, I might add.

This doc was in shock. I don't think he had ever come across a mother who was so ready to leave the hospital so quickly after delivering. He was a bit baffled, but he did look over little lady and saw that she was in perfect health. He asked all those questions about how many diapers she had gone through. Had she pooped yet? Was it that awful tar substance? Was I formula-feeding or nursing? How was nursing going? How long with my other girls before my milk came? There were so many questions. I honestly think that he was just trying to stall, trying to come up with some reason (other than policy) for not letting us leave the hospital, but he couldn't, and when I could tell that he could not possibly rack his brain for any more questions, he released us.

I was thrilled to be going home, to get into my own bed, to get into my own clothes, and, frankly, to get into my own undies. The hospital will supply you with several pairs of what they think of as panties. I will spoil it for you: they are in no way, shape, or form panties. Think of the absolute worst pair of granny panties. Like old-school granny panties—you know the ones that go all the way up to your belly button and cover your entire ass—then change out the material for a really thin burlap. And add a full-coverage pad. They call them pads, but they are just really small adult diapers you stick in those things they claim are panties. Yup, that is what you leave the hospital in. You too will be excited about wearing your own undies again.

I have to admit, the first six weeks with number three were much easier than with number two. If you have a really hard time with one, it can be different with the next. Whereas I was probably well past "baby blues" with baby number two when I was up crying all night, every night, with this one, there was not the weight of that. I was able to smile and actually be happy. When I laughed, it was really a laugh, not an act to make people think that I was okay. I was able to enjoy this time of having a newborn in the house. Moral of the story: Expect every experience with each child to be different. Experiencing baby blues with one by no means guarantees that you will have them with all your babies.

Baby number three was a happy baby, which also made things much easier. As long as her basic needs were met, she was up for taking over the world. And the other girls were old enough that they could go play together if Mommy needed a nap while baby was napping.

Although things were going well—and, frankly, easy compared to the other two—we rarely left the house until Hubby came home. The idea of getting all four of us dressed would wear me out: all the hair that needed brushed and pulled up. All the socks to find, then one who couldn't find one of the shoes that she had to wear that day. I would get completely worn out just getting everyone dressed. And forget about my hair and makeup—that was just not happening. I was happy if I was showered.

Then would come the whole circus of getting everyone into the car, and then everyone out of the car, plus trying to get anything done. It was just too much for me, so we waited for my loving and incredibly patient husband to get home to drive us wherever we needed to go.

This go-around, I had let my darling husband know right from the start that once baby girl was here, I was done working. That was right: D. O. N. E. Done with trying to keep up with everything at home and get it right at the office. There was simply no way that I could handle that load. With the experience that I had been given with my other two daughters, I had learned that the weight of that load would crush me. Knowing this was okay. Actually, that was great. I knew my limits this go-around. I knew that I was not going to be able to handle working and taking care of three kids and stay sane.

My very best advice on this topic is this: Find your limits, state them clearly, and don't get pushed over them. It is okay to stand up for yourself. It is okay to say that something is too much for you to handle. And it is okay to say no. It took me a very long time to learn that lesson, and even more time to put it in motion. Though I wanted to be the perfect mom who did it all, the perfect wife who could handle it all and still have dinner on the table, it was not possible. *My* definition of perfection had to change. Change = good. Change that is positive for your sanity = perfection.

I always knew that I was going to be a stay-at-home mom, from the time that I was a little girl. My image of a stay-at-home was very, very different than the path that we are on at the moment, however. In my imagination, I would be wearing an A-line dress, complete with pearls, making the kids a big breakfast before school, having lunch at the club with my girlfriends, then coming home in time to pick up the house, do a load of laundry, and have a full home-cooked meal on the table just in time for when my loving (and doting) husband walked in the front door. Can we cue 1950? That is what I saw.

While he always knew that I wanted to stay at home, as I never hid this fact and brought it up at every possible time while we were working together, it still surprised my husband. I think he was actually shocked when I told him that I had too much on my plate and it would be in the best interest of everyone at this point if I didn't return to work. With this being something that I had talked about since we had dated, and all through our more than ten years of marriage, I did not expect it to be any sort of fight or issue.

Once again, I was wrong. Oh, so beautifully wrong. He was not on board with this plan at all. He genuinely liked having me working with him. He loved building not only our family but also our business together. To him, it was a personal jab that I was ready to be done. So we split it right down the middle. Kind of.

He would handle all the business, except for those times when they were very short-handed or desperately in need of some help, and I would handle all of the things related to the house, minus the yard or the cars.

It took us a few years to work out the new balance of routines and workload, to get it right with us, without resentment. It is okay to disagree over working or staying at home. It is even okay to fight over these things. They are huge life-changing choices. If you fly through marriage without any issues or are on the same page on every choice, you should worry, because that, I promise you, is not normal. But as long as you are willing to work through it, as long as you are willing to walk in the other person's shoes to really understand where the other person is coming from, and listen to that point of view, things are good.

My days are nothing like those 1950s shows. I don't wear dresses every day, and certainly never with pearls. My house is not spotless and ready for company at the drop of the hat, unless you are family or a very close friend, 'cause then you know that I am a horrid housecleaner. Because we homeschool, my lunches at the club had turned in PB&Js around the coffee table.

A good day is a day when I get a shower in and my makeup on. Rare are the off days, or the days we know we are having company, when the kids are bathed and dressed in their "company clothes" (a.k.a. the cute clothes), the house is picked up, and I am dressed and put on. On those days when I am the perfect mom, it is all a sham, a show, a con. I will confess it is not real life and is most certainly not how it is every day, but shh! Don't tell anyone.

If you are like me, running around crazy with kids who are in their PJs till noon, a sink full of dirty dishes, and laundry that is piled higher than you stand, then welcome to the club. My name is Kat, and it's nice to have you here.

CHAPTER 12
Surviving Your First Emergency

Yup, an emergency is going to happen at some point. It is not fun, and it is stressful, even more so when it is your kid going to the ER. There is nothing good about this situation, except for the funny story that you can make it into, months or years down the road.

For the most part, an emergency for an injury that was self-inflicted will not be too life-threatening. Don't get me wrong, there are times when there is nothing funny about the situation then or now. There are times when it will be terrifying and you will wonder if you are going to make it through the night. Those are not the times or trips that I am talking about here. I am talking about the times when your kid does something, has an accident, that is too severe to wait for a doctor appointment but is not a we-won't-make-it-through-the-night type of event.

Okay, now that we have in mind what type of trip we are talking about, here are the steps to take to making it through that first, second, or hundredth trip to the emergency room. You need to take a big breath and relax as much as you can. I realize that when you have a child screaming in pain and you can physically see that something is seriously wrong, trying to relax is the very last thing that you want to do, but you need to. You cannot drive a screaming child to the hospital if you are shaking because you are so wound up. That might cause an accident on the way and make a bad situation worse. Also, if you are creating drama and stress, your kid will pick up on that and will cry, scream, and basically be even more hysterical. So calm down. Taking a few seconds for a deep breath or two is not going to cause problems in the long run, I promise you.

Once you're as calm as you can get, then really evaluate the issue. There is no need to pay for an ER trip when Urgent Care or even waiting for a doctor appointment will suffice. If a bone is sticking through skin, you need to go to the ER. A badly skinned knee can probably wait to see the doctor. If your child swallowed a button, you probably need to go to the ER. If your child swallowed a little bit of Vaseline, you can probably just call poison control or wait to see a doctor if you are that worried. The trick is to be calm enough to really assess a situation. For me, when in doubt, I go to Urgent Care. It's less expensive than the ER, but quicker than going to the doctor, and x-rays can be done at most Urgent Care locations.

Now that you have decided where to go, you need to get your other kids taken care of. You will need to be focused on the child who needs care. Plus, the hospital is a dirty place, so why risk taking everyone there if you don't have to? We leave one parent at home with the kids, and the other one goes with the child needing care. The parent who is at home will arrange for someone to come over to watch the kids if the parent at the hospital calls and says that it is serious enough that they both need to be there. Confused yet? Yeah, it is a bit confusing, and all of this will go down in a matter of minutes. It will test your Supermom skills.

Then you wait. You wait in the waiting room for your name to be called, you wait for a nurse to take vitals, you wait to be seen by a doc, you wait for test results, you wait for that doc again, and then you wait to be discharged—all with a screaming child who is overly clingy because he or she has no idea what is going on. Though you don't want to be the parent who is helplessly waiting at home for news, that job is way easier.

With any luck, that will be your trip to the ER. At least it was for us, both times.

When my oldest was about two and half or three, I was still working at the office most days. We had the cutest little office, and it was in a great part of town. It had state-of-the-art security, with all the bells and whistles. The doors were all heavy steel doors that automatically closed and that automatically locked once they were closed. It was just a push bar to unlock and open, so easy—unless you are a toddler who does not even stand as tall as that push bar, let alone have the strength to trigger it to unlock.

My husband and I were packing up the office, getting ready to call it a night, when we heard it—a loud thud. The front door had just dropped shut. Then it came: that scream, that cry, when you just know something is not only off but seriously wrong. I turned to see that somehow, my daughter had opened the door and then it had slammed shut on her hand, right in the middle of her palm. In fact, if we looked through the window, we could see her fingers on the other side of the door. I just knew she had crushed her hand. The steel door was completely shut and locked, with her hand stuck in it. I rushed over to get the door open and look at her hand. My husband diverted her attention by asking her lots of questions about what had happened and how she was feeling. If her poor hand had been crushed or mangled, we didn't want her to see it. Luckily, it was not mangled, but it was very bruised and starting to swell. She was having a hard time moving it at all.

Luckily, our office was always stocked with jumbo popsicles. They were the perfect size to lay in her cupped hand. We let her know that she needed to keep the popsicle on it until we were at the hospital and the doctor was ready to take a look at it. We figured that it would not only help with the swelling but would also block her view of her bruised black-and-blue hand.

Our office was right around the corner from an Urgent Care. We thought that that would be the way to go, because it was within walking distance and had an x-ray machine. Once we told the staff what had happened, we were taken right back. The doctor came in and actually went with us to x-ray so if it was crushed we wouldn't be waiting to hear that we needed to go to the ER.

I think I held my breath the entire time that we were there. It was far more scary than any time that I had been there for me. I was completely and utterly helpless; there was nothing that I could do. I couldn't make it go faster, I couldn't take away the pain, and I couldn't even hug her while she was in the x-ray room. While the whole process from when we entered the Urgent Care office to taking her x-ray, couldn't have been more than 15 minutes, they were the longest 15 minutes of my life.

The doctor looked at the results and smiled. He actually smiled at my daughter's crushed hand. Then he calmly walked over to my husband and me. "Nothing is broken. She will be sore for a few days, but she will be just fine." Relief swept through me like no other. How her hand had been completely shut in the door and was just fine, I have no idea, but I was going to take the news. We gathered her up, and off to get ice cream we went. Ice cream for dinner sound like the perfect type of treat.

My house was very quiet for the next few years. My oldest was to the point where she knew what not to do, and my middle child was too timid to try to do anything that might get her hurt. I liked those years, those years when we didn't have to wonder if it was okay just to go to Urgent Care or if we needed the ER. But all good things must come to an end, and my baby was the end of that bliss. She was a daredevil right from the beginning. There was no fear in her, and if her big sisters could joke about doing something, then by all means, that meant she could actually do it.

It certainly made for some interesting memories and even more interesting phone calls to poison control. We had their number on speed-dial. We called about her eating all of the baby Vaseline, her eating an entire tube of toothpaste, her eating the dog food. This child, we had to watch every single moment, and she kept us on our toes.

One evening, I had just gotten the little ones all bathed. The girls and I were in my room, drying off, getting their hair all brushed and braided—the normal items for when girls are out of the bath. I had my youngest go first. She was all excited that we were braiding hair, instead of blow-drying it so that way in the morning, she would have "Taylor Swift"—or as we called it, "T-Swift"—hair. Finally, we got her done, and I switched over to start doing my middle daughter's hair. Out of the blue, one of Taylor Swift's songs came on the radio. (What, you don't pump up the volume on the radio when you are bathing your kids?) My youngest got all kinds of excited, dancing her little butt off, getting into the groove, and before we knew it, her feet were moving faster than the rest of her. Then there she was, flying in the air.

Well, as you know, what goes up must come down. And she came down with all the grace of an elephant. It was not pretty. Then she started screaming. There was blood everywhere. We have baseboard heaters at my house—the kind that stick out of the wall about six inches from the carpet. They have a sharp edge and tiny corners. Mix that with a flying and then falling two-year-old, and you are asking for an accident. She managed to hit it, then slide along it, cutting a three-inch gash on her upper gums and biting her tongue at the same time.

She looked like a cartoon character; every time she opened her mouth, she was squirting blood. There was no need to discuss it. Since her gums were flapping open and the blood was not slowing, I picked her up, and off to the ER she and I went, in her pajamas, wet hair and all.

By the time we got there—mind you, we live in a small town, and it took us all of four minutes to get her in the car and to the hospital—her whole face was swelling and she had an awesome black eye going on. She was still screaming, so her PJs were covered in blood as well. The attendant took one look at her and whisked us straight back. There was no asking for my ID or my insurance. There was no paperwork to be filled out. Straight back to the exam room.

That was when I got scared. When do you go the hospital and they don't ask you for some form of ID? The nurse back there was great, though. Trying to hold little miss so she could get a good look was comical. The little girl was all kinds of pissed off, screaming her head off, squirting blood anywhere and everywhere she looked. The nurse was asking me to try to hold her more still. I am shocked that the nurse didn't get a finger bitten. By the time she was done trying to get a look, all three of us were covered in blood, but the nurse didn't think that any real trauma had been done. She gave my daughter bubbles to blow while we waited for the doctor.

That quieted her right down. She got to blow bubbles in the hospital way past bedtime. She went from screaming and spraying everything near her with blood, like in a cheesy horror movie, to a happy toddler blowing bubbles and humming to herself in a nanosecond. The only catch was that she had to keep gauze in her mouth so her blood could stay in her. She was just fine with that trade.

The doctor came in, took one look at her mouth, and told us there was nothing he could do for this type of injury and with this type of laceration, she would need to see a pediatric dentist first thing in the morning. Eight hundred bucks later and with a referral to the dentist, we were sent on our way.

Luckily, because this is a small town, the ER left a message for the dentist to say that we would be coming in. They knew exactly who I was when I called in, and they had us come right away.

There was no real damage done. She was going to have to eat only soft foods that she did not have to bite into for the next two weeks, and for just about that long, she was going to be sporting a black eye. Of course, the next day, we had a big family day trip planned, and she looked pitiful for all the pictures, but hey, if the worst part of the ER trip was a few bad pics, I will take it any day.

If you have kids, at some point, you will probably need to take them to the ER. Keep your cool, and look for the funny part of the story. It will all work out, mama.

CHAPTER 13

Be the A-Team: Be the Awesome Team

We have a saying in our family: "Just be awesome." It doesn't matter what you are doing or trying to do. Just be awesome. What that means is be your best, give it your all, jump into things with both feet, and lead with your heart. If you do those things, then there is no stopping you; you will be awesome.

So how do you become the Awesome Team? I mean, it is hard enough for any one person to be awesome and just worry about that awesomeness. Trying to be an awesome team? Talk about a tall order. For me, the Awesome Team (how many times can we fit that phrase into this paragraph?) is up to Mom and Dad. They need to be an awesome team, 'cause I promise you that once you have three or more, you are outnumbered. The children will find the weak spot; they will divide and conquer. Kids are way smarter and savvier than we give them credit for. They will push and prod until they find the single weak point in the chain, then they will exploit it for everything that it is worth. The kids, if you let them, will rule the roost—and let's be honest: while that is so much easier, it is not what you want. Kids who grow up like that are the adults no one wants to be around. All kids need structure; all kids need boundaries; all kids need to know what is expected of them. This is how they grow into contributing and successful members of society.

Part of being the Awesome Team is knowing your family, knowing what works for them or what doesn't, and then doing what works. Put your plan into motion. If your daily life is not working, then make baby steps toward what you would like to see or what you would like your day to be. My daily life might look completely different than yours. That is perfect, if your life is working for you.

No two families are the same, so what works for one might not work for another. Kelly down the street is totally stress-free, dancing through life with her toddler playing barefoot and her baby strapped to her back. She is loving life. To her, that is perfect, that is what is working. For my family, it would be complete and utter chaos. Does that mean her way is wrong and mine is right? Nope. Just two different paths that are working their own ways in two different families.

How do you know if your life is working or if you are just getting by? Well, there are a lot of little ways to know if it is working. Ask yourself these questions:

Am I yelling more than I want?
Do I have to ask my kids to do things more than once before they do it?
When I tell them that something will happen if they don't listen, do I follow through?
At the end of the day, am I happy and pleased with how the day went?
When we go out, do people comment about how well behaved my children are, or do they look the other way?
When my kids are playing with others, do they all get along, or do I have to play mediator?
Is this the way that I want my life to look forever?
Do my significant other and I fight about the kids?

If you are happy with all of the answers that you had to these questions, then go, you. You are part of the Awesome Team! Go pop open a bottle of wine and celebrate your awesomeness. If there were some that you would like to change, or ways that you would want to improve your family's routine, you have already started on a new plan. Finding what you want to change is one of the hardest parts, because you have to admit that it is not working as perfectly as you want. Once you see the change that you want to make, it is much easier to put a plan in motion.

I know my kids do so much with a set schedule every day. They do not like not knowing what is coming next. We are not fly-by-the-seat-of-our-pants people. Also, they need lots of sleep. So part of what my husband and I do is set up pretty tight schedules for all the kids. The schedules include the times that they get up, eat, school, snack, and so on. It might seem rigid to those who don't schedule a lot outside of doctor appointments, but for us, it is huge. Even going on vacation causes stress for the girls, since it is a change from that schedule. Ever hear a mom say she needs a vacation from her vacation? Yup, we are that family.

Here is our daily plan:

> Up by 7:30–8:00 (depending on how the night is and if they went to bed on time)
> Breakfast by 8:30
> School at 9:00
> Break for lunch from 1:00 to 3:00
> Extracurricular (Girl Scouts, swimming, or dance, depending on time of year) and Finish school if needed at 3:00
> Dinner at 6:30
> Teeth, PJs, and story at 7:30
> Lights out at 8:00

While it may seem boring to have everything so planned and mapped out, it helps keep the girls on task and keeps the anxiety at bay. Also, having this helps my husband and me be the Awesome Team. It is kind of our secret sauce to parenting. We both know the girls' schedule, so it doesn't matter which one of us is at home or working with the kids that day. It is a seamless transition. We don't rely on the kids to tell a parent what is up next. No wondering if we are missing something. Your significant other and you are a team, and when it comes to the kids, you guys have to be on the same page. A planned-out, boring schedule can help you do that.

You both also need to be on the same page not only when it comes to dishing out the discipline but alo what the discipline will be for each infraction, then on the same page about how to follow through with said discipline. There should be no "good guy," no "bad guy," no "easy parent" or "tough parent." Both parents should be equal. My kids know that it doesn't matter which one of us they come to, the reaction will be the same. Now, I may be slightly softer and more understanding, and my husband may be a bit more to the point, but they won't get a lighter punishment from me or a harder one from Dad.

What if you disagree with your partner's consequence? I mean, you are not the same person. You both have ideas and ideologies about parenting. There will be times when one parent is on the forefront of an issue or dealing with whiny kids all day and dishes out something that is so harsh or so far out of left field that it leaves the other parent wondering where that even came from. In the moment, the situation might have been completely overwhelming and your significant other might have gone to your plan A agreed-upon discipline action and it didn't work. Maybe the kids were far too overtired or

had too much junk food, and they just kept pushing those buttons and your partner snapped, "Fine, then we are going to throw everything away."
Yes, we had one of those moments. Then what?

In front of the kids, you need to support your partner's choice. You know it was an overreaction, you know that once your partner cool downs, he or she will regret it. You also know that once your partner cools down and you talk to him or her, the consequence will change. But in front of the kids, you need to support that over-the-top overreaction. You have to have your partner's back. None of this "Don't worry, sweetheart, I will go talk to Daddy," or "Don't listen to what your mother said. It is okay," or, even worse, disregarding what your partner has said altogether and going about your day as if nothing was said. By doing that, you are letting your kids know that you and your partner are not a team, that what one parent says has more weight than what the other says. Most importantly, it teaches your children that they can play you against each other. If they can get in between you, they will always divide and conquer.

How do you support each other? You point out to your child that he or she did something that is not acceptable and that there are consequences for acting inappropriately. You say that you are sorry that your child is upset but his or her actions led to whatever consequence was dished out. Children need to be taught that actions have direct reactions. Keep the conversation on the action that your child did, what made your child pick that path. Then have your child take accountability for that action. Once your child does that and is calmer, he or she may very well accept the consequence. If your child doesn't accept the consequence, just stick to your (or your partner's) guns.

Once the kids go to bed and the house is quiet, go talk to your partner. Explain to your partner why you think the consequence was over the top and where you think you should go from there. It should be a two-way conversation; you are not your partner's parent. There are no times when either party should be laying down the law and expecting the other to fall into line.

As long as you are listening to each other and supporting each other, you will be part of the Awesome Team. Find the balance that works well with your family. Find the schedule (or lack of schedule) that works well with your family. Find the solutions that work well with your family.

Are you seeing the pattern? Do what is best for your family, not what everyone else is telling you to do. Not what Meg the manicured mom is doing for her family, or what your grandma told you you should be doing. But listen to your partner, pay attention to your family, and listen to your gut. You will find what works best. Then just put that plan into motion with the rest of your team, and everything else will work itself out. I promise you!

CHAPTER 14
Happy Moments

Motherhood is one crazy ride, that is for sure. I don't think that you will ever meet a mom who will tell you any of these things:

"Oh, this is exactly what I thought it would be."
"Life is so easy all the time with kids."
"I never yell."
"My kids never throw temper tantrums in public."
"Every moment of every day is exactly what I want."
"I have never thought about running away with the circus."

Well, maybe that last one is just me, but on those days when the kids are determined to drive me bat-shit crazy, I daydream about running away with the circus and spending my days playing with the elephants.

If you ever meet a mom who says any of those things, just smile, nod, and know that she is flat-out lying to you—or on some seriously good drugs, and in that case, find out what they are. Then let me know.

So if this ride is as hard as any real mom will tell you, why in the world do we choose to do it? (It *is* a choice.) Why do we invest the majority of our lives into these little beings that test our sanity as well as our self-control? Let's face it: If we couldn't see those silver linings and all the reasons that we picked this path, it would be easy to get resentful, grumpy, and irritated.

We do it for those happy moments, for those moments in the day when we look at life and smile. The moments when our kids are all getting along. The moments when everything seems to be aligned. No matter how hard it is to see those moments, they come every day. Some days, you have to fight and really force yourself to see them, but they are there, if you look.

For me, those moments are when the kids get really quiet and I start to worry that they are getting into something, or doing something that they know that they shouldn't be doing. I go and search for them, and find them all snuggled up under the covers, reading to each other.

Or the moments when they are playing loudly with each other, and laughing, giggling, and talking fill the air, and no matter how loud I turn up the music, I just can't get over their noise—the happiness they have when playing with their siblings.

Or when I am washing the dishes after dinner and the girls jump right up on the counter to tell me all about their day: what so-and-so said, or what they are reading before bed. When they just want to spend time with Mommy no matter the menial task that I am doing.

Or at bedtime, and they ask for just one more story ("Please, just one more."), and I know full well that one more will turn into two more and then five, but they just want stay up with me.

Or when I check on them before I go to bed myself and find them fast asleep, snuggling with their stuffed animals, all safe and warm, dreaming about pirates or princesses.

If you are having a really hard day (we all have them), try to find your moments. Spend a minute or two remembering why you wanted to be on this ride. The hard days will always end; life has a way of moving on and getting better.

Those are the moments, the reasons why we choose to be moms, and why when people ask, we say it is the best job in the entire world. Would you really have it any other way? I know that I wouldn't.

Afterword

Thank you for reading my book. It means more to me than you will ever know that you took time out of your day to read it. I hope that it made you laugh, made you think, maybe shed some light on something going on in your life. Most of all, I hope that it made you realize that all those moms you think you are perfect aren't. They are going through the same issues that you are.

If you are wanting more, check out my blog at: www.confessionsoftheperfectmom.com

I love hearing other moms' stories so please connect and say hi. I personally respond to each and every message. I am looking forward to hearing from you.

Thank you again.
—Kat

CPSIA information can be obtained at www.ICGtesting.com
Printed in the USA
BVOW02s0846110915

417218BV00002B/88/P